# *WHAT* Not *HOW*

## The Business Rules Approach
## to Application Development

D0764644

# *WHAT* Not *HOW*

## The Business Rules Approach
## to Application Development

## C. J. DATE

## ADDISON-WESLEY

**An imprint of Addison Wesley Longman, Inc.**

*Reading, Massachusetts • Harlow, England • Menlo Park, California*
*Berkeley, California • Don Mills, Ontario • Sydney*
*Bonn • Amsterdam • Tokyo • Mexico City*

The publisher offers discounts on this book when ordered in quantity for special sales. For more information, please contact:

Corporate, Government, and Special Sales
Addison Wesley Longman, Inc.
One Jacob Way
Reading, MA 01867

Visit Addison-Wesley Professional on the Web: *www.aw.com/cseng*

**Library of Congress Control Number:**

00-131706

ISBN 0-201-70850-7

Text printed on recycled and acid-free paper.

1 2 3 4 5 6 7 8 9 10–MA–04 03 02 01 00
*First printing, April 2000*

# For my father, Henry

❖ ❖ ❖

*These simple little rules and few*
—Hilaire Belloc

*That to come*
*Shall all be done by the rule*
—William Shakespeare

*As if rules were not . . .*
*Derived from truth, but truth from rules*
—Samuel Butler

*"That's not a regular rule: you invented it just now."*
*"It's the oldest rule in the book," said the King.*
*"Then it ought to be Number One," said Alice.*
—Lewis Carroll

*Rules and models destroy genius and art*
—William Hazlitt

*The golden rule is that there are no golden rules*
—George Bernard Shaw

*He has observ'd the golden rule*
*Till he's become the golden fool*
—William Blake

*We never do anything well*
*till we cease to think about the manner of doing it*
—William Hazlitt

# Contents

❖ ❖ ❖

# Preface

❖ ❖ ❖

An exciting new technology called **business rules** is
beginning to have a major positive impact on the IT
industry—more precisely, on the way we develop and
maintain computer applications. The aim of this book
is to explain what this new technology is all about,
and why you should care.

I must make it very clear right away that the book is
not impartial. I'm very enthusiastic about business rules!—
and I hope you will be too, when you've finished reading.
In other words, this is definitely a book with an attitude:
It explicitly champions the business rules idea, and it
describes and explains what in my opinion are the merits
and benefits of that idea. Why am I so enthusiastic? For two
reasons: because of what the technology can do, and because
it is so squarely in the spirit of "the original relational
vision." And the book's structure reflects these two points.
To be more specific, Part I is an overview of what business
rule technology consists of and what it makes possible,
and Part II then takes another look at the ideas presented in
Part I and considers them from an explicitly relational point
of view.

I should also make it clear that the book grew out of the
script for a live presentation. As a consequence, the style is
a good deal chattier than my usual writing, and the tone is
possibly a little shrill on occasion . . . In the interests of full

disclosure, I must also explain that the presentation and the book were both produced under an agreement with Versata Inc. (formerly known as Vision Software Tools Inc.), a company that has a business rules product to sell. However, the book is not about Versata specifically, nor is it about any other specific company or product; rather, it's about business rule technology in general. What's more, "the views expressed are my own"; they're not necessarily endorsed by Versata, nor by any other vendor. Equally, I don't mean to suggest that all of the features we're going to be examining can be found in all of the commercially available products (or in some cases, perhaps, in any of them!). The book describes how business rule systems work in *general* and in *principle;* it doesn't necessarily correspond exactly to the way any given product works in practice.

**Who should read this book:**   Part I of the book is meant to introduce business rule technology to the widest possible audience. It's deliberately not very technical; in fact, it's intended primarily as a "manager's guide" to the subject, though I do believe that technologists, especially people concerned with developing databases and applications in the traditional way, should benefit from it as well. All you need in order to understand Part I is a basic knowledge of what databases and applications are all about, together with a broad idea of what's involved in the traditional approach to developing such databases and applications.

Part II of the book is a little more technical in nature, but not very much so; the primary target audience is still basically as for Part I, and in any case most of the technical background required to understand the overall message is explained in the text itself.

**How to read the book:**   Part I is meant to be read in sequence as written and in its entirety; skipping chapters or reading them in a different order is not recommended, at least not on a first reading. Part II can be skipped if you like, but if you do read it then I would strongly suggest, again, that you read it in sequence and in its entirety, at least on a first reading. Of course, the book is quite short, and you could probably read the whole thing in a single sitting if you felt like it.

**Acknowledgments:**   First of all, I'd like to thank the people at Versata (especially Mike DeVries and Val Huber) for supporting me in the writing of this book, and Gary Morgenthaler for suggesting that I write it in the first place. Second, I'd like to thank Manish Chandra, Paula Hawthorn, Keri Anderson Healy, Vi Ma, Rahul Patel, and Ron Ross for help with technical questions and the like during the preparation of the manuscript. Ron Ross in particular deserves a special mention for his persistence over the years in trying to make me buckle down and get my thoughts on this subject into some kind of order . . . Thanks, Ron! Third, I'm very grateful to my reviewers Hugh Darwen, Val Huber, Paul Irvine, Haim Kilov, Rahul Patel, Ron Ross, and David Wendelken for their generally enthusiastic and helpful comments on earlier drafts of the manuscript. Finally, I'm grateful, as always, to everyone at Addison-Wesley (especially Paul Becker and Ross Venables) for their encouragement and support throughout this project, and to my editor Elydia Davis for her usual sterling job.

C. J. Date
*Healdsburg, California*
*2000*

# PART I

# Overview

This first part of the book is intended for anyone who wants to gain an understanding of what business rules are all about at an overview kind of level. It's deliberately not very deep, technically speaking. It consists of eight short chapters, as follows:

1. What's the Problem?

2. Business Rules Are the Solution!

3. Presentation Rules

4. Database and Application Rules

5. The Data Model

6. Potential Advantages

7. Potential Disadvantages

8. Summary of Part I

The material is written on the assumption that you have at least a basic knowledge of what databases and applications are, and that you also have some general idea of what's involved in the traditional approach to developing such databases and applications.

# What's the Problem?

❖ ❖ ❖

When they first began to appear, in the early 1950s or so, computers were very hard to use—they required very specialized skills, and you really had to be a computer technician in order to use them at all; originally, in fact, you probably had to be a hardware engineer. Over time, however, computer systems have become much more "user-friendly" and easy to use, thanks to a continual *raising of the level of abstraction:* so much so, in fact, that now you can use a computer effectively even if you have almost no knowledge of how its internals work at all (much as you can drive a car effectively even if you don't know what goes on under the hood). Here are a few familiar examples of that "raising of the level of abstraction" that have taken place over the years:

■ 1GLs ⇒ 2GLs ⇒ 3GLs ⇒ 4GLs

Programming languages have evolved through several "generations," from first generation languages (1GLs) to at least a fourth generation (4GLs). Just to remind you: 1GLs were machine languages; 2GLs were assembler languages; 3GLs were the so-called "high-level" languages (COBOL, Fortran, and the rest); 4GLs were various proprietary languages, such as FOCUS from

Information Builders, Inc. Some people regard SQL as a 4GL [16].*

- Sequential files ⇒ indexed (ISAM) files ⇒ hierarchic and network databases ⇒ SQL tables

Over the years, more and more of the details of storing and managing data have been taken over by the system; in a word, they've been *automated*. Nowadays, it's the system, not the user, that's responsible for finding data as and when required (and finding it fast); it's the system, not the user, that's responsible for recovering data in the event of failure; it's the system, not the user, that's responsible for protecting data from concurrent update; and so on.

- Specialized languages and interfaces: for example, RPG, SQL, QBE, "visual programming" (QBF, ABF), spreadsheets, . . .

This one is more or less self-explanatory. However, I'd like to elaborate briefly on QBF and ABF, because they're directly relevant to some of the ideas we'll be examining in the next few chapters. QBF—*Query By Forms*—allows you to do database queries and updates[†] by making simple entries in a form on the screen. ABF—*Applications By Forms*—allows you to develop applications in the same kind of way, and those applications in turn also use on-screen forms as the interface with the user. *Note:* QBF and ABF both grew out of work originally done in the early 1980s at the University of California

---

*Throughout this book, numbers in square brackets refer to publications listed in the References and Bibliography section at the end of the book.

[†]In accordance with normal usage, this book uses the term "update" generically to include all three of the familiar operators INSERT, DELETE, and UPDATE.

at Berkeley [26]; they were first commercialized in the Ingres product, originally from Relational Technology Inc., now—under the name Ingres II—from Computer Associates International Inc.

Let me add a word on spreadsheets, too. Spreadsheets raised the level of abstraction, in their particular field of application, by getting away from writing programs *entirely* (nobody today would use Fortran to write an application to perform spreadsheet-style processing). There's a very direct parallel here with business rule systems, as we'll see.

In a nutshell, then, it should be clear that the historical trend has clearly always been away from *procedural* and toward *declarative*—that is, from **HOW** to **WHAT**. HOW means saying how, step by step, the work is to be *done;* WHAT just means saying what the work to be done *is.*

So why is this trend A Good Thing? The answer is, of course, that declarative (WHAT) means the system does the work, while procedural (HOW) means the user does it. In a nutshell:

## Declarative is better than procedural!

So wouldn't it be nice if we could do *all* of our application development work declaratively? Such has indeed been a goal for many, many years (people have been talking about the possibility of **fully compilable and executable specifications** ever since the 1970s, if not earlier [28]). In other words, wouldn't it be great if we could simply *specify* our applications precisely, and get the system to *compile* those specifications into executable code?

Well, we're getting there. As we'll see.

The advantages are obvious: *Productivity*, of course—the work gets done much more easily and much more quickly; and numerous subsidiary benefits follow, including in particular various kinds of *independence*. One familiar kind is *data* independence, which lets us make changes (for performance reasons, for example) to the way the data is physically stored on the disk, without having to make any corresponding changes in applications that use that data. And there are many other kinds of independence too, some of which we'll be looking at later in this book. The basic advantage in all cases is that they make applications immune to certain kinds of change (in particular, immune to certain kinds of *business* change). And that's a good thing, because—as we all know—the only thing that's constant in life is change.

But what exactly is an application? Obviously, it's the implementation of some business function—for example, "insert an order line item," "delete an order line item," "update the quantity on hand of some part." In general, an application involves three parts or components:

*Applications have three components*

1. **Presentation aspects**
2. **Database aspects**
3. **Aspects specific to the business function** *per se*

Presentation aspects are the ones having to do with the end-user interface—displaying forms to the end user, accepting filled-out forms from the end user, displaying error messages, producing printed output, and so forth. Database aspects are the ones having to do with retrieving and updating database data in response to end-user requests and end-user entries on forms (they're the portions that interact with the database server, also known as the DBMS). Finally, "aspects specific to the business function *per se*" might be thought of as the application proper—they're the ones that specify the actual processing to be carried out in order to implement the business function, or in other words the ones that effectively implement the business's policies and practices.

Now, of these three components, the first two have been largely automated for some considerable time. Application developers no longer write detailed code to paint screens or look for changes in forms on screens—they just invoke builtin *presentation services* to get those tasks done. Likewise, they don't write detailed code to manage data on the disk, they just invoke certain builtin *database services* to get *those* tasks done.

But the third component—the aspects specific to the business function *per se*—those are still mostly done "by hand," meaning that somebody typically still has to write a lot of procedural code. And, of course, that's the problem . . . **It's time to automate that third component!** And that's really what "business rules" are all about: *automating the business processing.*

The following back-of-the-envelope analysis might help to give some idea of the magnitude of what we're talking about. A typical database table might need, say, five pages of supporting procedural code; a typical database (not a large one) might contain 100 tables; a good hand-coder might produce a page of code per day. *Net:* 500 person-days for a hand-coded system. By contrast, simply *specifying* that same system might be a matter of, say, five or six weeks—and if those specifications are executable, then we've effectively reduced the development time by an order of magnitude.

As you can see, automating the business processing, if it could be done, really would be a quantum leap forward. (Sorry about the cliché, but I really do think what we're talking about here deserves the description—much more so, indeed, than certain other "quantum leaps" that have been much discussed in the past.) Writing procedural code is tedious, and time-consuming, and error-prone, and leads to the well-known application backlog problem, as well as many other related problems that we'll get to later. And the "in principle" solution to all of these problems is obvious:

**Eliminate the coding!**

That is, specify business processing declaratively, via business rules—and get the system to compile those rules into the necessary procedural (and executable) code. And just how we might actually be able to do this is the subject of the next few chapters.

Having set the scene, as it were, let me close this introductory chapter with a quote to support some of the things I've been saying. It's taken from an interview [15] with Val Huber of Versata Inc. (formerly known as Vision Software).

> **Years of experience with information system development have taught us two important lessons—it takes far too long to turn a relatively simple set of requirements into a system that meets user needs, and the cost of converting existing applications to new technologies is prohibitive . . . The factor underlying both of these problems is the amount of code it takes to build a system . . . If code is the problem, the only possible answer is to eliminate the coding by building systems directly from their specifications. That's what the rule-based approach does.**
>
> **—Val Huber**

As you can see, Huber is effectively suggesting, again, that what we should be aiming for is *compilable and executable specifications*. Observe in particular that he touches on two separate problems with the old-fashioned way of doing things:

- The time it takes to build applications in the first place;

- The difficulty of migrating existing applications to take advantage of new technologies as they become available (for example, moving a client/server application on to the Web).

I'll come back to both of these problems in Chapter 6.

# Business Rules Are the Solution!

2

❖ ❖ ❖

To repeat from Chapter 1, the problem we're faced with is, in essence, the problem of having to write procedural code. And business rules really are the solution to that problem, because they allow us to specify applications declaratively instead of procedurally.* As I put it in that chapter, business rules allow us to *automate the business processing.*

Let's take a closer look at what the business rules approach involves. Suppose we have a database involving customers and orders—more precisely, customers, orders, order line items, and parts—that looks like this:

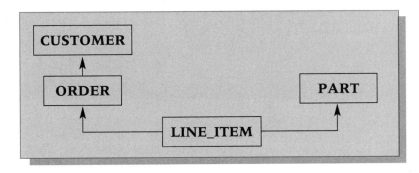

*The customers and orders database*

---

*By the same token, object technology is *not* the solution, in my very firm opinion. Object languages—Java, C++, and so forth—are still essentially just procedural programming languages (and so someone, somewhere, is still writing a lot of procedural code), and they seem to have little or no concept of declarative rules at all.

Just to be definite, let's assume this database is an SQL database specifically. Then the boxes in the figure correspond to SQL tables, and the arrows correspond to foreign keys that relate those tables to one another, logically speaking. For example, there's a foreign key from the ORDER table to the CUSTOMER table, corresponding to the fact that every individual order must be placed by some customer.

By the way, if you'd rather think of CUSTOMER and the rest not as SQL tables as such but rather as *entity types*, well, that's fine; in some ways, in fact, it might be better to talk in such terms, since they're not so specific. Business rules aren't specific to SQL databases! But I'll stick to SQL, for the reason already given.

Observe now that:

- Each customer has many orders (but each order is from just one customer); each order has many line items (but each line item belongs to just one order); each part is involved in many line items (but each line item involves just one part).

- The foreign key relationships can be thought of, in part, as *existence dependencies:* An order can't exist unless the corresponding customer exists, an order line can't exist unless the corresponding order and part both exist.

- Those existence dependencies are business rules! Indeed, foreign key constraints in particular are an important special case of business rules in general, and I'll have quite a lot more to say about them in Part II of this book.

Here then, in outline, are SQL definitions—that is, CREATE TABLE statements—for the four tables in the customers and orders database:

```
CREATE TABLE CUSTOMER
      ( CUST# . . . ,
        ADDR . . . ,
        CREDIT_LIMIT . . . ,
         . . . ,
        PRIMARY KEY ( CUST# ) ) ;


CREATE TABLE ORDER
      ( ORDER# . . . ,
        CUST# . . . ,
        PAID . . . , ----------------------------------------- yes or no
        SHIPPED . . . , ------------------------------------ yes or no
         . . . ,
        PRIMARY KEY ( ORDER# ) ,
        FOREIGN KEY ( CUST# ) REFERENCES CUSTOMER ) ;


CREATE TABLE LINE_ITEM
      ( ORDER# . . . ,
        LINE# . . . ,
        PART# . . . ,
        QTY_ORD . . . ,
        ORD_PRICE . . . , ----------------- fixed at time of order
         . . . ,
        PRIMARY KEY ( ORDER#, LINE# ) ,
        FOREIGN KEY ( ORDER# ) REFERENCES ORDER ,
        FOREIGN KEY ( PART# ) REFERENCES PART ) ;


CREATE TABLE PART
      ( PART# . . . ,
        CURRENT_PRICE . . . ,
        QTY_ON_HAND . . . ,
        REORDER_LEVEL . . . ,
         . . . ,
        PRIMARY KEY ( PART# ) ) ;
```

Some points to note regarding these definitions:

- The CUSTOMER table includes a CREDIT_LIMIT column, with the obvious semantics.

- The ORDER table includes two yes/no columns, PAID and SHIPPED, that indicate whether the customer has paid for the order and whether the order has been shipped, respectively.

- The LINE_ITEM table includes the part number (PART#), the quantity ordered (QTY_ORD), and the corresponding order price (ORD_PRICE). The order price is locked in at the time the order is placed and doesn't change, even if the current price of the part does subsequently change.

- The PART table includes the current price, the quantity on hand, and the reorder level, all with the obvious semantics.

- Finally, note that the PRIMARY KEY and FOREIGN KEY clauses correspond to business rules (and of course they're stated declaratively). For example, it's a business rule that every customer has a unique customer number; as mentioned earlier, it's also a business rule that every order involves exactly one customer; and similarly for all of the other primary and foreign key declarations.

Now let's consider a typical business function involving this database—"insert line item," say. The way it works goes something like this:

- By clicking on a menu item or something of that nature, the end user asks for a form corresponding to the LINE_ITEM table to be displayed on the screen.

- You can think of that form as a form in the style of QBF (recall that we discussed QBF briefly in the previous chapter): It will include among other things fields corresponding to the customer number, the order number, the part number, and the quantity ordered.

- The end user fills in those fields appropriately—that is, he or she provides the necessary information regarding the new order line—and clicks on "enter" or "save" or something of that kind.

The "insert line item" application is now invoked and carries out the following tasks (among many others, of course):

**A.** It checks the customer's credit limit.

**B.** It computes the order total.

**C.** It determines whether the part needs to be reordered.

A., B., and C. here are business requirements that must be met in order to carry out the overall business function. Incidentally, there's an important point here that I'll come back to in a little while (when I discuss *reuse*): Those very same business requirements might also need to be met as part of certain other business functions—for example, "change line item" or "delete line item." But let's concentrate on the "insert line item" function for the time being.

For each of these three business requirements, then, the application developer will have to specify a corresponding set of business rules. In the case of the "check credit limit" requirement, for example, the rules might look something like this (of course, I'm simplifying the syntax considerably, for obvious reasons):*

---

*It's worth mentioning that—as will quickly become clear—the process of developing these rules precisely mirrors the "analysis interview" process: The analyst gets the business user (a) to state the business objectives and (b) to provide definitions of terms that get introduced in step (a).

**1.** If TOTAL_OWED > CREDIT_LIMIT, reject

The meaning of this rule, obviously enough, is that the new line item must be rejected if it has the effect of carrying the total owed by this customer over the customer's credit limit. But what do we mean by "the total owed"? Clearly, we need another rule:

**2.** TOTAL_OWED = Sum ( ORDER_TOTAL where not PAID )

Note that there isn't any "total owed" column in the CUSTOMER table, so the total needs to be computed as indicated.

Observe now that this second rule refers to the order total. So this rule leads us directly into the second business requirement, "compute order total," for which the rules might look like this:

**3.** ORDER_TOTAL = Sum ( LINE_ITEM_AMOUNT )

**4.** LINE_ITEM_AMOUNT = QTY_ORD * ORD_PRICE

QTY_ORD and ORD_PRICE are both specified as part of the line item (the line item to be inserted, in the case of the "insert line item" business function), so LINE_ITEM_AMOUNT can be computed directly.

Finally, here's the rule for the third business requirement, "determine whether reorder is required":

**5.** If QTY_ON_HAND – QTY_ORD < REORDER_LEVEL, reorder

"Reorder" here can be thought of as the name of another application, part of the same overall integrated application system (or what we used to call the *application suite*). Alternatively—and this is a very important point—"reorder" might mean "send an email message to some external agency." So we're not just talking about calling subroutines!—and we're not just talking about applications in the classical sense. I'll have a little more to say on this point in Chapter 8.

As you can see, then, these rules are fairly declarative (nonprocedural). **But they can be compiled into procedural code.** In other words, the rules are executable (loosely speaking). So we've specified the application in a purely declarative way—we haven't explicitly written any of the usual procedural code at all—and yet we've still wound up with running code: an application that can be executed on the machine.

By the way, the procedural code produced by the compiler isn't just executable code—it is (or should be) *optimized* code as well. That is, the rules compiler is (or should be), specifically, an optimizing compiler. I'll have more to say on this particular point in several subsequent chapters.

That's the end of the example for now (though we'll be coming back to it at several points in the next few chapters). To repeat, we've just built an application without writing any procedural code! And there are many immediately obvious advantages that accrue from this way of doing things. Here are some of them:

- First of all, of course, the declarative rules replace many pages of hand-written procedural code. Each of those rules could easily correspond to a couple of hundred lines of 3GL code! This is the source of the productivity benefit, of course.

- Next, the rules are applied and enforced—"fired," to use the jargon—on *all relevant updates.* I touched on this point before, when I observed that the very same business requirements might need to be met as part of several different business functions. To be more specific, although the rules we looked at in the example were specified as part of the process of building the application called "insert line item," *they're relevant to other applications too.* For example, the application called "delete line item" should clearly also cause the rule "compute order total" to fire, *and so it does.*

To put the point more simply: The application developer doesn't specify *when* the rules are to fire, or what events have to occur in order to trigger them. (We don't want to have to specify those triggering events, for all kinds of reasons. One obvious and important reason is that we might get them wrong.) Rather, we simply say what the rules *are,* and the system itself—the "rule engine," as it's sometimes called—figures out when they should fire. Productivity!

■ It follows from the previous bullet item that there's no need for the application developer to get into the business of writing that complicated "on event" hand-code that's required with certain 4GLs. (It's relevant to mention too that those 4GLs were often still fairly procedural—not to mention proprietary—even when they were "event-driven," as it were.) And there's another point here as well: Not only is that "on event" hand-code difficult to write, it's also difficult to debug and maintain. What's more, the events in question tend to be, specifically, *database* events—for example, "when this record is updated"—rather than *business* events like "when an order line is entered."

*Note:* Actually the foregoing paragraph is slightly overstated. Sometimes we do effectively have to define "on event" rules after all. Rule 5 above, the reorder rule, might be regarded as a case in point; in that example, the triggering event is basically "when the quantity on hand falls below the reorder level" (though the rest of the rule can hardly be described as "complicated hand-code"!). Be that as it may, I propose to ignore such cases from this point forward, until we get to the discussion of *stimulus/response* rules in Chapter 5.

■ It also follows from the previous bullet item that rules are automatically *shared* across applications and *reused* across applications. It's rather like the situation with the database itself: The data in the database is also shared and reused across applications, as we all know. And the advantages of such sharing and reuse for rules are analogous to those for sharing and reuse for the data itself. In effect, just as the relational model originally allowed us to integrate, share, and reuse *data,* so business rule technology allows us to integrate, share, and reuse *applications* (or pieces of applications, anyway).

■ Another advantage of declarative rules is what might be called the "single-level store" advantage. To be specific, the rules make no mention of any kind of artifical boundary between the database and main memory; data is data, wherever it resides, and there's no need to move data out of the database and into main memory in order to process it. (No need so far as the user's concerned, that is. Of course the data does have to be moved under the covers. But why should the user care? Let the system do it!)

■ Finally, note that the rules can be stated *in any sequence.* To say it another way, we have *ordering independence* for the rules. Business rule technology allows us to get away from the tyranny of the von Neumann architecture, which forced us to think everything out in a highly pro-cedural manner, one step at a time. As Gary Morgenthaler has said [21]:

[With the business rules approach,] programmers . . . are freed from the burdensome task of having to redefine their business problems in the deadening pursuit of stepwise instructions for the program counter.

Down with the program counter!

Of course, the procedural code that's compiled from the rules does have to pay attention to the program counter (the rules do have to fire in some well-defined sequence). So how is it done? How does the rule engine figure out that sequence? Basically, it does so by means of what's called a *dependency graph*. In the example:

1. In order to check the credit limit, the system needs to know the total owed;

2. In order to compute the total owed, it needs to know the line item amounts;

3. In order to compute the line item amounts, it needs to know the line item quantity and price. But it does—these values are given by columns in the LINE_ITEM table (or are provided by the end user, in the case of a new line item that's currently being inserted).

So the dependency graph shows that 1. depends on 2. and 2. depends on 3.—so (obviously enough) the system fires the rules in the sequence 3., then 2., then 1.

By the way, note the reliance in the foregoing on the foreign key constraints (which are rules too, of course, as we already know). For example, the rule

TOTAL_OWED = Sum ( ORDER_TOTAL where not PAID )

implicitly makes use of the foreign key from ORDER to CUSTOMER (the order totals to be summed for a given customer are precisely those for orders that have a foreign key relationship to the customer in question). *Note:* Foreign keys can also be referenced explicitly, of course, where such explicit reference is necessary.

I'll have more to say regarding the advantages (and potential *dis*advantages) of the business rules approach in Chapters 6 and 7. For now, I'd like to close this chapter with a brief remark on the question of terminology. The fact is, the term "rules" might be convenient, but it's hardly very precise, or even very descriptive. After all, we already deal with all kinds of rules in the database world, or the application world, or both. Here are a few examples:

- Security rules

- Integrity rules

- Codd's "12 relational rules"

- Foreign key rules

- BNF production rules

- Type inference rules

- Armstrong's functional dependency rules

- Expression transformation rules

- Logical inference rules

I'm sure you can provide many more examples of your own.

What's more, the same goes for the term "*business rules*" as well; that term also is neither very precise nor very descriptive. Note in particular that not all enterprises are businesses! But it doesn't seem to be easy to come up with any better terms—at least, not ones that are so succinct—so I'll go with the flow in this book and stick with the term "business rules" (which I'll abbreviate to just "rules," usually). However, the key point is really **declarativeness;** the important thing is really that we're talking about a *declarative* technology, not a procedural one.*

So what does the term "business rules" cover? In this book, I take it to include all of the following (but be warned that not everybody uses the term in exactly the same way):

---

*However, to quote Paul Irvine, who reviewed a preliminary draft of this book: "The term *business rules* gives the concept a very marketable tag . . . *declarative programming* just won't sell!" A sad comment but undoubtedly true.

1. Presentation rules

2. Database rules

3. Application rules

In other words, rules apply to all three aspects of applications as identified in Chapter 1. In the next couple of chapters, we'll take a closer look at each of these three kinds of rules.

# Presentation Rules

3

As noted in Chapter 1, the presentation aspects of applications have been reasonably well automated for some time now. For that reason, presentation rules should be fairly familiar to you, so I'll be brief here.* Basically, what happens is this:

- Suppose we have some table in the database (or some entity type, if you prefer); let's just call it *T*.

- Then we need to tell the rule engine, somehow, that *T* exists. I'll come back in Chapter 5 to the question of how we might do this.

- The rule engine will then build a QBF-style form (plus supporting internal code, of course) for table *T*.

- Now that form can be used as a basis for formulating queries and updates, and displaying query results, that involve table *T*.

---

*Another reason to be brief is that many people tend not to include such rules under the general heading of "business rules" anyway. But there are good reasons for defining presentation rules, as well as database and application rules, at the rule engine level; in particular, as noted later in this chapter, greater uniformity and consistency of forms across applications is thereby facilitated.

For example, suppose *T* is the CUSTOMER table from the database in the previous chapter. Then:

- The corresponding form will have fields for the customer number, the address, the credit limit, and so forth.

- If the end user wants to find (say) all customers with credit limit less than $500, he or she can simply enter something like "< 500" in the credit limit field and click on "enter" or something.

- The corresponding customers can then be displayed, one at a time, using the same form (there'll be some kind of "Next" button that allows the end user to scroll through the customers one by one).

What's more, that same form can, and will, be used in every application that needs to support such interactive access to customers—another example of sharing and reuse across applications (here it's the form that's being shared and reused, of course, along with its supporting internal code).

Moreover, that same form can be made part of the predeclared *workflow sequence* for the overall application; that is, appropriate form *transitions* can be defined, through some interactive "boxes and arrows" kind of interface. The resulting boxes-and-arrows diagram effectively represents the overall application at a high level of abstraction; to be specific, it shows the sequence in which the constituent actions need to be performed. (Despite the negative remarks regarding ordering and procedurality in previous chapters, sequence isn't *always* bad! In a restaurant, you can't eat the meal before it's brought to your table.)

The next point is that the form can now be *customized* in a variety of ways. Here are some examples of the kinds of things that can be specified (and hence the kinds of things that can be customized):

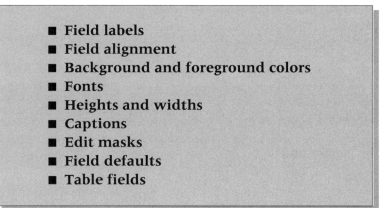

- **Field labels**
- **Field alignment**
- **Background and foreground colors**
- **Fonts**
- **Heights and widths**
- **Captions**
- **Edit masks**
- **Field defaults**
- **Table fields**

Most of these are fairly self-explanatory, except perhaps for the last one, "table fields." The idea here is simply that, for example, the customer form might include a table or "repeating field" listing all orders for the customer in question. That table will be separately scrollable, of course.

By the way, this repeating field example touches on a more general (and important) point, as follows. I mentioned *form transitions* a few moments back. Well, those form transitions, like the repeating field example, will often be based on certain *foreign key relationships.* For example:

- It's extremely likely that the application user, after calling up a particular customer form on the screen, will wish to see all orders for that customer (either as a table field on the customer form or as distinct forms).

- Analogously, it's extremely likely that the application user, after calling up a particular order on the screen, will wish to see all line items for that order, either as a table field on the order form or as distinct forms.

In both of these examples, and many others like them, the system can automatically determine the next form to be displayed, thanks to its knowledge of primary and foreign keys. In other words, the overall application can be perceived from a high-level point of view as a collection of forms and legal transitions among those forms, and foreign key relationships have a large role to play in defining (and automating) those legal transitions and supporting that high-level perception.

Here are some more sophisticated examples of presentation rules that might make sense for the customers and orders database:

- Customers whose accounts are overdue must be displayed in red.

- Rush orders must be displayed before regular orders.

- Line items for a given order must be displayed in part number order.

And so on.

Anyway, the really important point in all of the above is that the presentation rules all ultimately "hang off" **the data model**—as indeed do all of the database rules and all of the application rules, as we'll see in Chapter 5. It follows, therefore, that the data model is *crucial* and *central* and *fundamental,* and we need to take a careful look at it. And we'll be doing exactly that in Chapter 5. First, however, we need to say more about the database and application rules, and that's the purpose of the next chapter.

# Database and Application Rules

4

❖ ❖ ❖

Frankly, it's hard to draw a sharp dividing line between database rules and application rules. In this book, therefore (and in this chapter in particular), I plan to treat them together. The following figure shows a rough classification scheme or taxonomy for such rules. It's based on, though not identical to, one given by James Odell in reference [19].

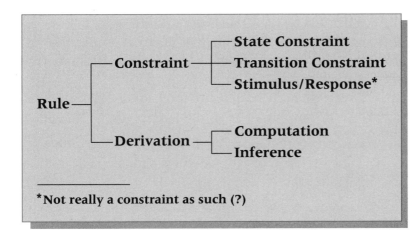

*Odell's rule taxonomy*

As you can see from the figure:

■ Rules are divided into *constraints* and *derivations*. (Odell's taxonomy does not include presentation rules.)

- Constraints are divided into *state* constraints, *transition* constraints, and *stimulus/response* "constraints." *Note:* The reason for the quotation marks in the last case is that stimulus/response "constraints" are really rather more than just constraints as such, as we'll see in a moment.

- Derivations are divided into *computations* and *inferences.*

I'd like to say in passing that Part II of this book describes a more precise (and in my opinion more useful) taxonomy than this one, but this one will do for now.

Let's take a closer look at this scheme, with some examples. First of all, then, constraints. What's a constraint, anyway? Basically, a constraint—also known more specifically as an *integrity constraint*—is a conditional expression that MUST evaluate to *true.* (If it doesn't, the operation that caused it not to is rejected—loosely, the update is undone—and an error message is sent back to the end user. That error message is specified when the constraint is specified; typically, it will consist of that very same constraint, expressed in natural language for reasons of user-friendliness. For example, the error message for the constraint TOTAL_OWED ≤ CREDIT_LIMIT—see below— might be something along the lines of "total owed *total* can't be greater than credit limit *limit*," where *total* and *limit* are the applicable amounts.)

As already indicated, there are three kinds of constraints, namely state, transition, and stimulus/response constraints:

- A *state* constraint defines legal "states" or values of the database. In terms of the customers and orders database, an obvious example is:

```
TOTAL_OWED ≤ CREDIT_LIMIT
```

A state of the database in which this condition is not satisfied is not a legal state.

- A *transition* constraint defines legal "transitions" or changes from one legal state to another. The customers and orders database as so far discussed doesn't involve any transition constraints, but a simple example from a personnel database might be:

```
new SALARY ≥ old SALARY
```

—"salaries can never decrease" (wishful thinking, perhaps).

As a matter of fact, transition constraints are quite common in the real world. In a database concerning people, for example, there might be a number of transition constraints having to do with changes of marital status. In such a database, the following transitions would all be valid—

- Never married to married
- Married to widowed
- Married to divorced
- Widowed to married

(and so on), whereas the following would not—

- Never married to widowed
- Never married to divorced
- Widowed to divorced
- Divorced to widowed

(and so on).

- A *stimulus/response* constraint is, as already mentioned, not really just a constraint as such (it's certainly not just an expression that's supposed to evaluate to *true*). Rather, it's a combination of a *triggering event* (that's the stimulus) and a *triggered action* (that's the response). For example:

```
ON DELETE CASCADE
```

In this simple and familiar example, the triggering event is execution of a DELETE operation, and the triggered action is "cascading" of that DELETE to applicable referencing rows.

As you can see, therefore, a stimulus/response "constraint" is really just what's usually—albeit sloppily—called a *trigger*. As such, it begins to look just a little procedural (although the particular example just shown is in fact still 100 percent declarative). While undoubtedly necessary, such "constraints" do open the door to what might be called *creeping procedurality:* that is, the temptation to write lots of rules in this form, which moves us away, somewhat, from the idea of specifying everything in purely declarative style. In Chapter 2, we saw that one advantage of the business rules approach is that there's no need to get into the business of writing that complicated "on event" hand-code—but triggers do move us back in that direction, somewhat. Note in particular that if two distinct "stimulus/response" rules have the same stimulus—that is, the same triggering event—then we might find ourselves getting into the business of having to specify the sequence in which the corresponding responses are performed . . . and now we're on a very slippery slope. (To repeat, I'm not saying stimulus/response rules are unnecessary—I'm just saying they need to be used with all due caution, and perhaps sparingly.)

Here's another example of a stimulus/response rule (this one applies to the customers and orders database):

```
If QTY_ON_HAND — QTY_ORD < REORDER_LEVEL, reorder
```

*Note:* This is as good a place as any to point out explicitly that business rules are much more than "just triggers." Critics of the business rules approach have been known to argue that everything that can be done with business rules can equally well be done with the conventional trigger mechanism. Quite apart from the fact that this claim itself is highly debatable—getting the trigger code correct can be very difficult, and implementation limitations often get in the way, too—the fact remains that triggers in general still mean that someone, somewhere, is writing a lot of procedural code. If the problem is that the system fails to provide proper declarative support for some functionality that clearly could be supported declaratively, the solution isn't to provide a way to implement that functionality procedurally!

Now let's turn to derivations. There are two kinds, computations and inferences.

- A *computation* rule is what it says—a rule, or formula, for computing one value from others. For example:

```
LINE_ITEM_AMOUNT = QTY_ORD * ORD_PRICE
```

- An *inference* rule is a rule that allows us, given certain facts, to infer additional facts. For example, given the facts "Anne is the mother of Betty" and "Betty is the mother of Celia," there's an obvious inference rule that allows us to infer that Anne is the grandmother of Celia. Or, getting back to the customers and orders example, we might have an inference rule that allows us to infer that certain customers are "good" customers:

```
IF TOTAL_PAID(c) > $100000 THEN GOOD_CUSTOMER(c)
```

("if customer *c* has paid more than $100,000 in total, then customer *c* is a good customer"; I'm assuming here that TOTAL_PAID is a column in some table somewhere, or alternatively is defined by means of some other rule somewhere). Note that this rule is effectively a *definition* of a good customer.

Having explained the basic idea, I'd now like to introduce some more examples for purposes of future reference. In some ways, these examples are (deliberately, of course) rather more probing than the ones we've looked at so far. If you have access to a commercial business rules system, you might want to see if that system can handle them! I mean, can you even *express* these examples in that system? If not, then somebody's going to have to write some procedural code once again . . .

These additional examples are all based on the well-known suppliers and parts database. Here's an SQL definition for that database (in outline):

```
CREATE TABLE S ---------------------------------- suppliers
       ( S# . . . ,
         SNAME . . . ,
         STATUS . . . ,
         CITY . . . ,
         PRIMARY KEY ( S# ) ) ;


CREATE TABLE P ------------------------------------- parts
       ( P# . . . ,
         PNAME . . . ,
         COLOR . . . ,
         WEIGHT . . . ,
         CITY . . . ,
         PRIMARY KEY ( P# ) ) ;


CREATE TABLE SP ----------------------------- shipments
       ( S# . . . ,
         P# . . . ,
         QTY . . . ,
         PRIMARY KEY ( S#, P# ) ,
         FOREIGN KEY  ( S# ) REFERENCES S ,
         FOREIGN KEY  ( P# ) REFERENCES P ) ;
```

As you can see, first, there's a *suppliers* table S, with
supplier number {S#} as primary key and some other items
(supplier name, status, and city or location). Second, there's
a *parts* table P, with part number {P#} as primary key and
some other items (part name, color, weight, and city or
location). And third, there's a *shipments* table SP, which
shows which suppliers are shipping, or supplying, which
parts in which quantities. The primary key for shipments
is the combination {S#,P#} of supplier number and part
number (because there's an assumption that there can't be
more than one shipment of any given part by any given
supplier at any given time). Note that shipments can be
thought of as a relationship between suppliers and parts:
a many-to-many relationship, to be more specific. Note also
the foreign key declarations.

By the way, there's nothing wrong with using more user-friendly names such as SUPPLIER, PART, and SHIPMENT in place of the rather terse names S, P, and SP used above. However, we'll be referring to these three tables so frequently in what follows that, rightly or wrongly, I felt it would be better to stick to very short names. Long names tend to become irksome with much repetition.

Here then are some possible (albeit rather contrived, in some cases) business rules that might very well apply to this database. Note that, in terms of Odell's taxonomy, they're all constraints specifically.

- Legal supplier numbers are of the form S*nnnn* (*nnnn* = up to four decimal digits).

  This first one is basically a *domain* constraint, in relational terms. We'll take a closer look at domain constraints in Chapter 11 (in Part II).

- Red parts weigh less than 50 pounds.

  This one is self-explanatory. But note that it's of a particularly simple form: It can be tested for a given part by examining just the row for the specific part in question *in isolation*—it isn't necessary to look at any other row in the parts table, nor at any other table in the database. Rules like this one are sometimes called *single-row* rules.

- Suppliers S1 and S4 are always in the same city.

  This fairly simple—and not at all unrealistic—example can be quite difficult to deal with in some systems. Observe that it involves examining two distinct supplier rows at the same time, and thus might be called a *multi*-row rule.

- No shipment quantity can be greater than twice the average of all such quantities.

  This one involves *aggregates* (averages, to be precise), and comparisons between such aggregates. It involves examining lots of rows "at the same time" (a multi-row rule with a vengeance!).

- Every London supplier supplies part P2.

This one involves the *universal quantifier,* FORALL ("for all" or "for every" or "for each").* It also involves two tables, the suppliers table and the shipments table (so it's not just a "multi-row" rule, it's a "multi-*table*" rule). *Note:* The other common quantifier is the *existential* quantifier, EXISTS ("there exists" or "there is"). An example of a business rule involving the existential quantifier might be "There exists at least one London supplier who supplies part P2."

- Suppliers in Athens can move only to London or Paris.

This is a transition constraint, involving just one table.

- Supplier cities and part cities are disjoint.

Another one that's easy to state in natural language but might be hard to express in some systems! It involves two tables, the suppliers table and the parts table, and it says that no supplier city is the same as any part city (or the other way around, if you prefer).

- Average shipment quantities never decrease.

This is a transition constraint involving aggregates (though only one table). *Note:* The constraint as stated is, deliberately, not very precise. It's supposed to mean "the average quantity of any given part, taken over all suppliers, can never decrease." The example illustrates the point that rules are indeed often stated rather imprecisely on a first cut. Refining them to make them precise is, exactly, part of the overall process of application or database development.

We'll revisit the foregoing examples in Part II of this book, in Chapter 11.

---

*Actually, most constraints—not all—involve FORALL; it's just that the involvement is particularly obvious in the constraint in question ("*for all* suppliers, if the supplier is located in London, then that supplier must supply part P2").

# The
# Data Model

In Chapter 3, I said the data model was "crucial and central and fundamental," and we needed to take a careful look at it. That's the purpose of the present chapter.

The first thing I need to do is head off at the pass a confusion that might easily get in the way of understanding otherwise. The fact is, the term "data model" is unfortunately used in the database world with two very different meanings, and we need to be clear as to which of those two meanings we intend in any particular context. The first is the one we have in mind when we talk about (for example) the *relational* data model. It can be defined as follows:

> **Data model** *(first sense):*   **An abstract, self-contained, logical definition of the objects, operators, and so forth, that together make up the abstract machine with which users interact**

*Note:* I'm using the term *objects* here in its generic sense, not in the special, rather loaded, sense in which it's used in the world of "object orientation."

And then—very important!—we can usefully go on to distinguish the notion of a data model as just defined from the associated notion of an *implementation,* which is defined as follows:

> **Implementation:   A physical realization on a real machine of the components of the model**

For example, consider the relational model. The concept *relation* itself is, naturally, part of that model: Users have to know what relations are, they have to know they're made up of rows and columns, they have to know what they mean (that is, how to interpret them), and so on. All that is part of the model. But users don't have to know how relations are physically stored on the disk, how row-and-column values are physically encoded, what indexes and other access paths exist, and so on; all that is part of the implementation, not part of the model.

Or consider the concept *join.* The join operator is part of the relational model: Users have to know what a join is, how to invoke a join, what the result looks like, and so on. Again, all that is part of the model. But users don't have to know how joins are physically implemented, they don't have to know what optimizations take place, they don't have to know what access paths—indexes and so on—are used; all that is part of the implementation, not the model.

In a nutshell: The model (in the first sense of the term) is *what the user has to know;* the implementation is what the user *doesn't* have to know.

(Just to elaborate for a moment: Of course, I don't mean to say that users aren't *allowed* to know about the implementation. They might indeed know something about it, and conceivably they might even use the model better if they do, but—to repeat—they don't *have* to know about it. The car driving analogy from Chapter 1 applies again: You might drive better if you know what goes on under the hood, but you don't *have* to know what goes on under the hood in order to be able to drive in the first place.)

Now let's turn to the second meaning of the term *data model*, which can be defined as follows:

> **Data model** *(second sense):* **A model of the persistent data of some particular enterprise**

The customers and orders (and so forth) model we were using as a basis for examples in earlier chapters is a data model in this second sense. *Note:* By the term *persistent data* in the foregoing definition, I just mean the data in the database (other writers sometimes use the term to mean something slightly different).

There's a nice analogy here which I think illuminates the relationship between the two meanings under discussion:

- A data model in the first sense is like a programming language, whose constructs can be used to solve many specific problems, but in and of themselves have no direct connection with any such specific problem.

- A data model in the second sense is like a specific program written in that language—it uses the facilities provided by the model (in the first sense of that term) to solve some specific problem.

Having now, I hope, clarified the distinction between the two meanings of the term *data model,* I can now be explicit and say that throughout Part I of this book, at least, I'll be using the term in its second sense, meaning a model of the data of some particular enterprise or business. (In Part II, by contrast, I'll be talking about the relational model specifically, so there I'll be using the term in its other sense. But first things first.)

All right: With that important preliminary out of the way, let me now say again that the *data model* (second sense) *is crucial!* We've already seen in Chapter 3 that the presentation rules "hang off" the data model, and we're about to see that the database and application rules do so as well (as is in fact fairly obvious). Thus, the data model really is the place to start. (Well, actually, the whole process is iterative, as we'll see in Chapter 6, but we do have to start somewhere, and that "somewhere" is the data model, or at least the first version of the data model.) To elaborate:

- First of all, business functions are expressed in terms of "business entities," such as customers, orders, and parts.

- Once again I'm going to assume SQL for definiteness. So those business entities map to rows in SQL tables (or, rather, the business entity *types* map to SQL tables as such*). Hence, business rules, which are the formal specification(s) of those business functions, are expressed in terms of those SQL tables.

  Incidentally, when I say "SQL tables" here, I don't necessarily mean just base tables. To be more specific, some entity types map to *views*. This fact will become important in Part II of this book, but I don't want to discuss it any further at this juncture.

- So we need to pin down the SQL tables first (unless this has already been done, of course); in other words, we need to carry out the logical database design process first.

The output from the logical database design process is, of course, the data model (second sense). And then we need to tell the rule engine about that data model somehow. Typically, we might do this by "importing" the model from the database catalog into the rule engine. The rule engine will then know what tables exist, what columns they have, and so forth.

---

*Actually, it would be more accurate to say those entity types map to SQL table *types* rather than to SQL tables as such—but the concepts of table and table type are bundled together in SQL. The distinction (which is perhaps not all that important for the purposes of the present book) is clarified in references [7] and [9].

(Indeed, the table definitions, column definitions, and so forth that together make up the data model can themselves—as already hinted but not stated explicitly in earlier chapters—be regarded as business rules too, even though they weren't included in Odell's taxonomy as discussed in Chapter 4.)

By the way, I do assume that all of the usual principles of good design are followed in the database design process: the principles of normalization, orthogonal design, and so forth [7]. After all, those principles certainly still apply, even if we're in this brave new world of business rules. Beware of anyone who tries to tell you they don't! The problems caused by bad design—data redundancy, update anomalies, and so on—still arise, even if applications are built declaratively (as indeed should surely be obvious).

And now I run into a small problem . . . The following is one of my favorite quotes:

> The gap between theory and practice is not as wide in theory as it is in practice [*anon*].

The point is, we're getting into an area where the "relational" vendors—well, the SQL vendors, at any rate—really didn't do a very good job, in my opinion. Indeed, I think they seriously let us down, by failing to deliver on the full promise of relational theory. As I've said elsewhere (see, for example, reference [7]), relational theory is *not* just theory for its own sake—the point of that theory is so that we can build systems that are *100 percent practical.* Every detail of that theory is there for solid practical reasons. And from the standpoint of relational theory, it's clear that business rules (with the possible exception of presentation rules) should surely be *part* of the data model, not something built on top of that model as an afterthought. Indeed, in an ideal world, those rules would be supported directly by the DBMS, not by some separate frontend software component.

However, we don't live in an ideal world, and so we have to fill in the gaps—gaps in the commercial SQL products, I mean—in whatever way we can. Hence there are good pragmatic reasons, at least, for not specifying rules as part of the data model *per se* but instead specifying them separately, and supporting them separately, via some separate frontend component. For the remainder of Part I, therefore, I'm going to assume that this is indeed exactly what we're doing. But I'll come back and say more about this issue in Part II of this book.

So the working assumption is that the rule engine is indeed a separate software component, independent of the DBMS and running on top of the DBMS, as the following figure suggests:

*Rule engine vs. DBMS*

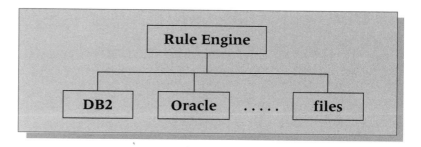

In fact, we can make a virtue out of necessity here and plausibly argue that the separation between the rule engine and the DBMS is actually an advantage, because it implies that applications can be *DBMS-independent* (which is, indeed, another important kind of independence). They can even span DBMSs, and/or various legacy systems—even file systems, possibly, as the figure indicates: another point I'll come back to later, in Part II of this book. *Note:* By *spanning DBMSs* here, I mean the application can behave as if it were dealing with a single database, even if that "single database" maps to any number of physical databases under the covers (see Chapter 13).

Now, I've alluded several times to the fact that rules are compiled into executable code. In other words, the rule engine includes a *rules compiler,* whose purpose is to convert the declarative rules into executable code that runs on top of the backend—or backends plural, perhaps, as mentioned above. What I didn't stress before, however, was the point that it's important for performance reasons that the rules in fact *be* compiled, not interpreted. (Some writers refer to this distinction as "early *vs.* late binding.") What's more, as noted in Chapter 2, the rules compiler can and should be an *optimizing* compiler—it can and should produce optimized compiled code. And when I talk of optimization in this context, one thing I mean in particular is that the system can automatically *partition the compiled code* appropriately across the client/server architecture, or three-tier architecture, or whatever architecture happens to be in place. "Automatically" means the human developer doesn't have to do it! The general objective should be to partition the code in such a way as to minimize—or at least reduce—network and I/O traffic. In particular, data-intensive processing should be done at the database server, not at the client (a state of affairs that's sometimes referred to as "thin client").

# Potential Advantages

6

❖ ❖ ❖

Now that you have some idea of what the business rules approach is all about, let's take a closer look at some potential advantages of that approach—and, in the interests of fairness, some of the potential *dis*advantages too. The present chapter is concerned with advantages, the next with disadvantages.

Let me begin by admitting right away that the points that follow are all very much interwoven. Sometimes they're even the same point in different guises (it's always hard to structure this kind of material completely orthogonally). Anyway, here goes.

The first point is that the business rules approach makes hardware and software resources more directly available to end users. End users can readily understand declarative rules, certainly much better than they do more traditional approaches to application development. They can even, sometimes, develop applications on their own, or perhaps with just a little help from IT professionals. As a consequence, the people who advocate the business rules approach often tend to be end users (business professionals) rather than "techies," though IT professionals certainly appreciate the advantages too.

And a related point: Business rules offer a way to capture business knowledge in a form that is independent of specific applications and specific implementation environments. This is another very important kind of independence: It means not only that rules can be shared and reused across applications, as we saw in Chapter 2, but also that they can be shared and reused across *environments*. As Ron Ross says in his "Declaration of Rule Independence" (in reference [24]): "Rules are basic to what the business knows about itself . . . Rules, in the long run, are more important to the business than hardware/software platforms." Right on!

To pursue the point a little further: Actually, I would argue that the complete set of business rules constitutes a **model** of the entire business.* That model is a technology-independent—and *time*-independent—specification of what the business does, and it truly is one of the business's most valuable assets. *It's the whole business at a glance*—"a good way to think about the business," as it were.

And another big point: By eliminating the code, we eliminate what some people, at least, would claim is *the principal source of errors*. With the business rules approach, applications are effectively "correct by construction," and the prime source of software instability simply goes away.

And yet another related point: Once the application has been developed and brought into existence, it automatically becomes interoperable with others. In effect, it becomes another building block that's available for incorporation into other applications, and invocation from other applications. In other words, we're talking about *extensibility,* or *application reuse* (the applications in question serving as what some writers call "components").

Now I'd like to focus in on the specific issue of rule sharing and rule reuse. Suppose the following business rule—actually an integrity constraint—applies to the suppliers and parts database from Chapter 4:

> *Suppliers with status less than 20 must not supply any part in a quantity greater than 500.*

---

*The term "model" is one of the most overworked in the whole IT industry, but in this case I think it's justified.

Formally, this rule might be expressed as follows:

```
IF S.STATUS < 20 AND S.S# = SP.S# THEN SP.QTY ≤ QTY(500)
```

("if the status of supplier S is less than 20 and supplier S has the same supplier number as shipment SP—meaning that shipment SP is a shipment by supplier S—then shipment SP had better have a quantity less than or equal to the quantity 500").

Now, if we had to implement this rule the old-fashioned way, by writing procedural code, we would have to include such code in at least all of the following routines (or procedures, or "methods," or applications, or whatever you want to call them):*

■ *The routine for creating a new shipment*

This code would have to say: Does the new shipment have a quantity greater than 500? If so, does the corresponding supplier have status less than 20? If so, signal an error.

■ *The routine for changing a shipment quantity*

And this code would have to say: Is the new shipment quantity greater than 500? If so, does the corresponding supplier have status less than 20? If so, signal an error.

■ *The routine for changing a supplier status*

This code would have to say: Is the new status less than 20? If so, does this supplier have any shipments with quantity greater than 500? If so, signal an error.

---

*One reviewer of a draft of this book pointed out that these routines at least would—or should—"be server code, not client code." True enough; but the fact remains that doing things the old-fashioned way means that somebody has to write a lot of procedural code, with all of its attendant problems.

■ *The routine for assigning a shipment to a different supplier*

And this code would have to say: Does this shipment have quantity greater than 500? If so, does the new supplier have status less than 20? If so, signal an error.

(Of course, I make no claim that this list of four routines is exhaustive—they just happen to be the "obvious" ones, the ones that leap to mind immediately. There might easily be others that need to do the same kind of checking as well.)

Given all of the foregoing, there are certain obvious problems that arise straight away:

1. We've clearly lost the possibility of the system determining for itself when to check and enforce the particular rule in question.

   As we saw in Chapter 2, with declarative rules, we don't tell the system *when* to do the checking, we simply tell the system what the checks *are* (except in the case of stimulus/response rules, which are best used sparingly anyway). In the case at hand, we wouldn't have to tell the system what updates it has to monitor in order to enforce the constraint, we would just have to tell it what the constraint is. To repeat a point already made in Chapter 2, we don't want to have to tell the system when to do the checking; quite apart from anything else, we might get it wrong. Instead, we want the system to determine for itself when to do the checking. And of course it can; there's an algorithm that, given the formal (declarative) expression of a constraint like the one in the example, lets the system figure out what INSERTs, what UPDATEs, and what DELETEs it has to monitor in order to enforce the constraint [2].

2. How do we ensure that all necessary routines include all necessary enforcement code? And ensure that all access is via those routines?

On the first of these two questions, you're on your own!—the system can't help you. And if you miss a routine, well, tough. On the second question, well, it might be possible to use the system's security mechanism somehow—but you'd better not forget to do it, for otherwise you might find that some updates effectively bypass the constraint, and hence bypass the checking.

3. If the constraint changes, how do we find all routines that need to be rewritten?

Observe first of all that constraints do change from time to time—they're just "business rules," and business rules change all the time, for all kinds of reasons. For example, think of the tax laws, which change every year (and the tax laws are basically just one huge, very complicated, business rule).
   So rules do change, and hence with procedural rule enforcement you're going to have to rewrite the routines that do the enforcement. And how do you know which routines those are? Good question! Again, you're on your own—and woe betide you if you miss one.
   In a declarative system, by contrast, it's easy to find all the rules that apply to some particular table (or some particular entity type)—you just do a query on the database catalog, or something equivalent to that catalog. Of course, in a declarative system, you don't have to rewrite the enforcement routines anyway, you just have to change the declarative rule(s).

4. How do we ensure the enforcement code is correct?

Once again, you're on your own—and if it isn't correct, well, again, tough. (Of course, it might not be correct in a declarative system either, but if it isn't, at least you know who to blame!—it's the *vendor*. And you'll probably get the fix pretty quickly, and a workaround too while you're waiting for the fix.)

5. How do we query the system to find all constraints that apply to a given table or combination of tables?

I've touched on this point already. In a declarative system, you just query the database catalog or equivalent. In a procedural system, you're on your own once again.

6. Will the constraints be enforced during load and other utility processing?

For performance reasons among others, utilities like load often have their own privileged, highly protected, low-level interface to the system (where the term "low-level" refers to the fact that the interface in question is below the regular user interface, which is basically at the SQL level). So the question is: Will those utilities bypass the constraints, if constraint enforcement is done at the regular user interface level? And the answer is, of course, that it's at least possible that they *will* be bypassed. Indeed, it's virtually certain they will be, if they're enforced via user-written procedural code and hence not even known to the system.

In a declarative system, by contrast, there are ways for the system to manage this problem, even if utilities do bypass the constraints. One technique is described in reference [11].

*Note:* I don't mean to suggest that bypassing constraints during utility processing is necessarily undesirable; on the contrary, sometimes there are good reasons for doing so. All I mean is that the process needs to be managed and controlled appropriately.

7. What about *semantic optimization*—making use of integrity constraints to simplify queries?

This is a big item. I'll come back to it in just a moment.

**8.** What about productivity, both during application creation and during application maintenance?

This is a big item, too, and I'll come back to it later as well.

Before I elaborate on these last two items, I'd like to summarize the other six points. Overall, the ability to state rules declaratively instead of procedurally means among other things that:

- We can avoid *redundant* rule enforcement. We don't have to have "the same" enforcement code embedded in lots of different chunks of procedural code or lots of different routines (or "methods," or whatever we call them). We just state the rule once, and the system does the work.

- We can avoid *inconsistent* rule enforcement. If "the same" enforcement code has to be embedded in lots of different routines, there's always the possibility that the enforcement code isn't really "the same" after all in all of those different routines. But with declarative rules, again, we just state the rule once, and *the system does the work.*

- We can't *forget* to enforce the rule. Again, if "the same" enforcement code has to be embedded in lots of different routines, there's always the possibility that the enforcement code isn't in fact included at all in some of those routines. But with declarative rules, once again, we just *state the rule,* and it's enforced automatically at all relevant times . . . **The system does the work.**

- Finally, the rules are kept in some kind of repository (perhaps the database catalog) and can be queried there. Compare what you have to do to find out what the rules are, and where they're enforced, in a procedural system (I've talked about this point at some length already, and I'm going to touch on it again in Chapter 7).

At this juncture, I think it's worth emphasizing the point (already made in Chapter 4) that *triggers aren't the solution* to problems like those identified above. Not only are triggers basically still essentially procedural in nature, but the procedural code in question can be very complicated indeed. As one reviewer (Paul Irvine) of an early draft of this book observed in connection with some triggers he had implemented himself: "The trigger code for implementing a certain business rule on just a single column was hundreds of lines long . . . It had to handle INSERTs, UPDATEs, DELETEs, and foreign key changes that logically moved a child row from one parent to another . . . To make the code generic took over a month, and each individual column still involved tens of lines of trigger code." (I've paraphrased these remarks slightly here.)

Now let me get back to the question of semantic optimization. Suppose we have a constraint on the suppliers and parts database to the effect that all red parts must be stored in London. Consider the following query:

*Find suppliers who supply only red parts and are located in the same city as at least one of the parts they supply.*

This is a fairly complicated query. However, if you think about it a little, you can see that:

- If the suppliers we want supply only red parts, then all the parts they supply must be stored in London;

- And if the suppliers we want must be located in the same city as at least one of the parts they supply, then those suppliers must be located in London.

So the overall query can be simplified—*dramatically* simplified—to the much more reasonable form:

*Find London suppliers who supply only red parts.*

And when I say "simplified" here, of course, I mean "simplified *by the system*"—I'm not talking about something the user has to do, I'm talking about something the system (actually the system optimizer) can do in the user's behalf, automatically.

*Terminology:* The query simplification we've just been looking at is an example of a *semantic transformation,* and the overall process of applying such transformations is called *semantic optimization* [17]. Semantic optimization can thus be defined as the process of using integrity constraints to simplify queries. The transformations are said to be semantic because they're ones that—in general—are not valid when considered from a purely syntactic point of view, but are in fact valid because there's an integrity constraint in effect that makes them so. In other words, if the original query is Q1 and the transformed version is Q2, then Q1 and Q2 are guaranteed to give the same answer only because there's an integrity constraint in effect that makes it possible to give such a guarantee.

Semantic transformation is such a great idea! The payoff from such transformations could be orders of magnitude greater than that from conventional optimization—partly because the transformation is done so early in the optimization cycle. However, I mustn't mislead you: I'm not aware of any database products on the market today that actually do very much in the way of semantic optimizing. But I do believe they'll do so in the future. And, of course, the crucial point is that the whole idea is critically dependent on the notion of being able to state constraints declaratively. Indeed, this is one of the reasons why doing things *relationally* is such a good idea. In a relational system:

- The constraint is basically an expression of the relational algebra (or something equivalent), and

- The query is also basically an expression of the relational algebra (or something equivalent), and so it's conceptually straightforward to combine the two into one big expression (and then go on and simplify that expression, and eventually evaluate or execute it). See Part II of this book, also reference [7], for further discussion of such matters.

Anyway, to repeat, semantic optimization is crucially dependent on stating constraints declaratively—so, if we do have to state them procedurally instead, by means of user-written procedural code, we've just shot ourselves in the foot. *Declarative is better than procedural!*

Finally, as promised, I want to come back and take a closer look at the issue of productivity. There are two facets to that issue—productivity during initial application development, and productivity later on during application maintenance. Let's take them one at a time.

- First of all, there's surely no question that initial development can be done dramatically faster with the declarative approach. We wouldn't expect anything different. It's just like the improvements you get with a 3GL over assembler language, or SQL over ISAM— though quite possibly a *bigger* improvement than in those cases; some early users of business rule technology have claimed anywhere from a five- to a fifteen-to-one reduction in initial development time. *Note:* The "single-level store" advantage discussed in Chapter 2 is of help in this connection.

- What's more, we're not just talking about "RAD" ("rapid application development"), which has been a fashionable buzzword for some time, of course. Rather, we're talking about what we might call "RID"—rapid *iterative* development. (Perhaps that "R" should stand for *responsive* rather than *rapid?*) With business rules, we can build an application that's at least approximately correct very quickly and show it to the end user immediately—not just the interactive forms, but the entire running application. And the end user can then react "in real time," as it were, and help the application developer iterate and get the application fully correct. To say it another way, we're talking about very rapid *prototyping*, and hence the possibility of involving the end user "in real time" in the application development cycle (which was hardly possible with older approaches, of course—certainly not to the same degree, at any rate).

The net effect of all of the above is that we can get applications up and running—and *correct*—much more quickly. And if the application supports some business service—as it presumably does, because otherwise why were we building it in the first place?—then we can make that business service available to the users or customers much more quickly too ("improved time to market").

One specific consequence of the foregoing is that third-party software vendors can build software products faster and more cheaply—perhaps underbidding their competition, too. Again, improved time to market.

All of this translates into *seizing new business opportunities as they arise,* instead of, as so often in the past, being held up by the IT department (or possibly even being completely stymied by the IT department, a state of affairs far from unknown in the past, in my experience).

Let me turn now to the issue of productivity during subsequent maintenance. Ron Ross [25] has pointed out that businesses today are faced with an "accelerating rate of change . . . Businesses currently are challenged by a variety of factors to be more adaptable than ever before." In particular, they must be able to change *applications* fast. And business rule technology makes this possible, of course, because:

- If some business policy or applicable regulation changes, we can just change the rule or rules and then recompile (*business adaptability*).

- If a business wants to take advantage of a new hardware or software platform, or a new architecture (such as moving from a centralized mainframe to client/server, or from client/server to the Internet), we can just reoptimize to that new environment (or recompile and reoptimize, more likely). This *deployment adaptability* is made possible by yet another important kind of independence (or, rather, several new kinds of independence) that the business rules approach provides—hardware independence, operating system independence, transaction monitor independence, DBMS independence, and so on.

The following figure compares this "new, improved" way of developing applications—the business rules approach—with the old "unenlightened" way of doing the same thing:

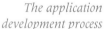
*The application development process*

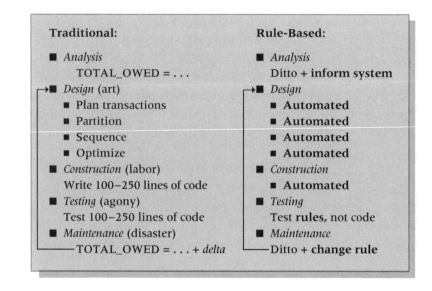

As the figure indicates, we can sum up the application development cycle as *analyze,* then *design,* then *build,* then test . . . then "*maintain*"—meaning there's a change in requirements, which takes us back to the beginning again, or at least back to design. And we go round and round this loop over and over again. In the figure, the (rather trivial) application simply involves "computing total owed," so the analysis is not very difficult. Be that as it may, traditionally we would then have to go on and figure out how that application is to be divided up into transactions; how the code is to be partitioned across client and server, or whatever the supporting architecture happens to be; what sequence those transactions must be run in; and how best to implement them. *All of this activity is automated with the business rules approach.* Traditionally, we would then have to write the code—it might be a couple of hundred lines, and it involves a very labor-intensive effort on the part of a person or persons with highly specialized skills. *This step is automated too with the business rules approach.* Next we have to test . . . This step isn't automated with the business rules approach, but it's much easier, because we're essentially testing algorithms at a much higher level of abstraction (we're testing the rules, not the code, as the figure says).

*Then the requirements change!* . . . For example, the formula for computing total owed might have to include some new delta, say freight or shipping charges. With the traditional approach, we're more or less back to square one. With the business rules approach, the same is true, of course, but the whole cycle is so much simpler. In effect, we just change the rules appropriately—perhaps just add a new rule, or change an existing rule—and do it all over again. No problem.

Adding or changing (or deleting) rules as just discussed is easy to do because of what might be called *rule independence*. To be more specific, each individual rule is independent of all the rest, at least insofar as such independence is logically possible. For example, suppose we have a system with 100 rules already, and now we need to add a new one. Well, we can simply add it at the end—we don't have to worry about its logical place in some sequence, because the system will figure out (a) if and how the new rule is related to existing rules, and accordingly (b) just what sequence the rules need to fire in. (This all works because of the dependency graph idea discussed in Chapter 2, of course.) To repeat the quote from Gary Morgenthaler in that chapter [21]:

[With the business rules approach,] programmers . . . are freed from the burdensome task of having to redefine their business problems in the deadening pursuit of stepwise instructions for the program counter.

So *rule independence* is yet another very important kind of independence that is enabled by the business rules approach.

# Potential Disadvantages

# 7

❖ ❖ ❖

It wouldn't be fair in a book of this nature to overlook the fact that the subject under discussion might have a downside too. Thus, we really ought to examine some possible disadvantages of the business rules approach as well, and try to understand whether they're real and whether we really need to worry about them, or whether they're at least something we might want to watch out for in a less than perfect implementation of the business rules idea. Hence the present chapter.

The first possible disadvantage that critics will point to is, of course, *performance*. Why am I not surprised? Well, to answer my own rhetorical question, I'm not surprised because this objection is always raised when we try to increase the level of abstraction. For example, it was certainly raised when Fortran, the first 3GL, was first invented in the mid 1950s (1954–1955). Indeed, the Fortran team at IBM—John Backus *et al.*—were so sensitive to the performance issue that they bent over backward to do a good job of implementation. And they were so successful in this regard that some of the techniques of compilation and optimization that they invented are still in use today.

The same thing happened when relational database technology first came along. Critics said, yes, we do need data independence, for all the well-known reasons, but data independence means late binding (interpretation), and late binding means bad performance. And so the System R team at IBM—Raymond Lorie in particular deserves the credit for this particular innovation [18]—showed that you could have data independence, and a high-level data language, namely SQL, and yet still have early binding (compilation) and good performance. Again, some of the compilation and optimization techniques that Lorie and his colleagues invented at IBM are still in use in SQL products today (and not just IBM products, either).

Turning now to business rule technology specifically, the solution to the performance "problem" (in quotes) with the still higher level of abstraction that business rules provide is once again basically *compiling and optimizing*—and I've already discussed these issues, somewhat, at several points earlier in this book.* (Of course, it's true that some implementations are likely to do a better job on these matters than others. I'm not saying you shouldn't worry about the performance issue. You *always* need to worry about the performance issue. But what I am saying is "Don't worry *too much*." Don't assume ahead of time that performance will be a showstopper.)

Another possible disadvantage is that—at least at the current stage of development, and with the current state of the IT industry—adopting a business rules product almost certainly means you're going to have to learn and use a new and proprietary language. Of course, we've heard this criticism before, too . . . My own response is that:

- First, Fortran and SQL, for example, were both proprietary languages at one time! And in any case:

- Any declarative business rules language is basically just **predicate logic,** or something very close to predicate logic. And migrating from one syntax for predicate logic to another, if it should ever be necessary, really ought not to be too much of a big deal. Certainly it shouldn't be as much of a deal as migrating from COBOL to Fortran,

---

*It's relevant to mention here that optimization—meaning, of course, *automatic* optimization, optimization that's done by the system, not by the user—is only feasible if user requirements are stated at a sufficiently high semantic level in the first place. It can't be done at all if those user requirements are embedded in hand-written procedural code. (These remarks were always true of relational database systems [7], and they're at least equally as true of business rule systems as well.)

or possibly even from one dialect of SQL to another. In any case, maybe we should be starting to think about some kind of business rules *standard?*

By the way, even if the input language is proprietary and nonstandard, the output language—the language into which the rules are compiled—can still be standard (for example, SQL and/or Java). This observation might be relevant to anyone who has to write hand-code to take care of features not (yet) supported by the business rules system at hand. For example, see the discussion later in this chapter regarding transitive closure.

The fact that the business rule language might be proprietary naturally touches on the question of the "learning curve" for the product in question. This point is somewhat product-dependent, of course; however, the learning curve really ought not to be too steep, for essentially the reasons articulated above (as well as other reasons given in earlier chapters).

Here are some more items to think about, perhaps rather more detailed ones. You could call these issues "potential disadvantages" too, if you like, but I think it's more reasonable to regard them as *opportunities* . . . because there's a good chance that a business rules system could actually do a better job in these areas than an old-fashioned application development system could. (Perhaps we should call them *future requirements?*) Anyway, let's take a look.

The first point is that, as we've seen, all of these business rules depend on the data model. So what happens if the data model changes, after the application has been built?

Well, first of all, the application will probably need to be changed too. This might mean just a recompilation . . . but is that recompilation automatic? Or does the application developer have to do something "by hand" in order to make it happen? And if it's not just a recompilation—if it means revising some of the rules first—does the system warn the developer that such is the case? Or does it just execute the application anyway, and perhaps give some kind of run-time error?

Such considerations might seem a little alarming at first sight. *But consider the alternative* . . . If you'd been developing applications the old-fashioned way, then you'd probably be much worse off—certainly you wouldn't be any *better* off—if the data model changed than you would be with the business rules approach.

The next question is: If the system *is* smart enough to do an automatic recompilation—or, at least, to attempt to do an automatic recompilation—when the data model changes, is it also smart enough to recognize when such recompilation is logically unnecessary? For example, when the change to the data model involves something that ought to be "transparent," such as adding a column to a table? If not, there could be extra overhead at the time the change is made.

Again, however, consider the alternative . . . The same arguments as before apply here, obviously; again, you can't possibly be any worse off in this regard than you were when you were developing applications in the old-fashioned way, and there's a good chance that you might actually be better off.

Next question: Are redundant rules (or subrules) optimized away? Here's a simple example: Suppose we have one rule that says salaries must be positive, and another that says they must be at least $3,000 a month. Then the second rule clearly implies the first, and there's obviously no need ever to check the first. What would *your* system do?

*Note:* This simple example illustrates the general point that *some constraints imply others.* And if constraint *A* implies constraint *B*, it would be nice if the system understood that enforcing *A* is sufficient to enforce *B*—meaning that *B* need not be explicitly enforced at all. Now, we obviously don't want the developer to have to be responsible for recognizing such a situation and deciding that *B* doesn't even have to be stated in the first place; we'd like the system to take care of matters for us automatically. In other words, we shouldn't be penalized for stating redundant rules. (Especially if rule *B* already exists, and then we add rule *A*. It should be clear that such a situation could easily arise in practice. For example, consider what happens if new legislation is introduced to increase the minimum wage.)

Once again, however, *consider the alternative:* If the two rules are enforced in two different applications—or even in the same application—via procedural code, then detecting the redundancy and "optimizing it away" will have to be done by hand, and very likely won't be done at all. In the business rules case, by contrast, it should at least be possible for the rules administrator (to invent a new profession on the fly) to query the rules repository and spot such redundancies as might exist. For example: "Show me all constraints that apply to employees." It's unlikely that the same kind of thing would be possible in a traditional system.

Another kind of redundancy that seems quite likely to occur in practice is the use of the same subexpression within two or more distinct rules. As a simple example, we might have one rule that says that total pay is equal to salary plus commission plus bonus—

```
PAY = SALARY + COMMISSION + BONUS
```

—and another that says that commission plus bonus must be less than five thousand dollars—

```
COMMISSION + BONUS < $5000
```

And it would be nice if the system would factor out the common subexpression and compute the value of COMMISSION + BONUS once, not twice. Again, we don't want it to be the developer's responsibility to do that factoring out ahead of time (because if it is, we begin to get back into the realms of "creeping procedurality" once again, if we're not careful).

Yet again, however, *consider the alternative:* Even if the system doesn't do a very good job of eliminating or reducing such redundancies automatically, the job of finding them and getting rid of them by hand is much easier than it would be in a traditional system, thanks to the fact that it's easy to ask queries about the rules.

Here's another issue: What about cycles or conflicts in the rules? Are they detected? If not, what happens?

- An example of a *cycle* might be where two computational rules define two quantities $A$ and $B$ in terms of each other—for example, $A = B + C$ and $B = A + D$. The system should be able to detect such cycles easily enough, because they'll lead to loops in the dependency graph. (If it doesn't detect them, of course, you'll discover them for yourself soon enough, because your application will run for a very long time!)

- An example of a *conflict* might be where we have one rule that says that salaries must be at least $3,000 a month and another that says they can't be more than $2,000 a month. Detecting (and resolving) such conflicts is difficult, in general—in part because they might involve any number of rules (and when I say it's difficult, I mean it's difficult for humans as well as for the system). If $N$ rules together lead to a conflict, then there's no way, in general, of deciding automatically which of those $N$ rules are valid and which invalid; the best you (or the system) can do is throw out the whole lot and say "There's a conflict here, but I don't know exactly where the problem is." The point is, determining where the problem is will depend on some additional information, information that, by definition, the system doesn't have (if it did, it wouldn't be additional). In the example, the additional information might be the knowledge that the rule that says salaries can't be more than $2,000 a month is now obsolete and needs to be dropped.

  Let me remind you, though, that even if the system doesn't detect conflicts for you, it does at least support rapid application development. So you'll discover very fast (if there's a conflict) that certain applications or certain updates always fail . . . meaning that you'll at least discover that there is a conflict very fast. Then asking queries about the rules should help you—or the rules administrator—to pinpoint the problem quickly.

  I'll say it one last time: *Consider the alternative!*

While I'm on the subject of potential disadvantages, I suppose I need to raise the question (perhaps I should have raised it right up front): Is it always possible to develop applications 100 percent declaratively, anyway? In principle, the answer to this question is certainly *yes*. In a real system, however, there are likely to be limitations. For example, the system simply might not provide—or (perhaps better) might not *yet* provide—all of the primitive operators that might be needed in order to be able to state all of the rules declaratively. There's a familiar example here: In the relational model as originally formulated (and in SQL likewise), there was no primitive operator for computing transitive closure. So SQL products typically require you to write a procedural program to do things like bill-of-materials processing (part explosion and so forth). But there's no reason why a suitable primitive operator can't be added to the relational model (and to SQL). Indeed, in some recent work of my own* (going by the name of *The Third Manifesto* [9], and discussed further in Part II of this book), I've done just that—added such an operator to the relational model, that is—and the new SQL standard called SQL:1999 (previously known as "SQL3") also includes some transitive closure support [16].

*Note:* Another situation in which some degree of procedural coding will almost certainly be required (at the time of writing, at least) is conventional batch processing. Here again, however, it could be argued that the need for procedural programming is due more to a lack of functionality in existing business rule products than it is to anything intrinsic. As a matter of fact, various "business-oriented" 3GLs and 4GLs didn't do too bad a job at raising the level of abstraction required for dealing with batch (I have in mind here languages such as IBM Corp.'s RPG and Informatics Inc.'s Mark IV).

Let me elaborate briefly on this question of possibly having to write some amount of procedural code. The point is, no software product is ever finished—they grow all the time to include ever more functionality, as we all know. Thus, it's not reasonable to expect the rule engine, or any other piece of software, to do absolutely everything you might ever want it to do—especially not in the first release! I think a reasonable objective would be for the rule engine initially to meet 80 percent of requirements (it's the old 80:20 rule, in fact; that is, 80 percent of the work you would otherwise have to do procedurally you should be able to do via rules). And, of course, that'll mean you'll be able to do *100* percent of some applications via rules. And then we have

---

*Done jointly with Hugh Darwen.

to hope that as the rule engine goes from release to release (and strength to strength), so you should be able to do more and more of the complete application development task via rules (that *has* to be the ultimate goal), and you should need to write less and less procedural code.

Of course, if you do have to write some procedural code, then you're effectively implementing a new operator . . . and once you've done it, then you should be able to invoke that new operator in other rules! In other words, you should be able to extend the system in arbitrary ways. What's more, such user-defined extensions should be preserved across system changes; they shouldn't be lost if (for example) you recompile some existing application, or if you upgrade the rule engine to some newer release.

The final "potential disadvantage" I want to discuss is this: Surely a strong argument can be made that all of this rule support we've been talking about ought to be in the DBMS anyway? Certainly people have talked about declarative DBMS support for *integrity constraints* for years. So do we really want and need the rule engine as a separate software component? Shouldn't the functionality really be a native part—an integral part—of the underlying DBMS instead?

What's more, if the rules are enforced in a separate rule engine and not in the native DBMS, aren't there bypass problems? That is, what happens if a user accesses the DBMS directly, thereby bypassing the rule engine? Might it not be possible to do some updates without having the applicable integrity constraints enforced, for example?

My own answer to all of these questions is both *yes* and *no. Yes,* because there's certainly some merit to the points being raised (as in fact I've hinted from time to time in what I've said in earlier chapters, especially Chapter 5)—and that's an issue that I'll be covering in some depth in Part II of this book. *No,* because there are also persuasive arguments in the opposite direction—in particular, the DBMS independence argument (the idea that the rule engine might run on top of many different DBMSs, maybe even several at the same time). Again, I'll be discussing such matters in more detail in Part II.

# Summary
# of Part I

8

❖ ❖ ❖

We've now reached the end of Part I of the book (the overview part), more or less. Just to review briefly, what I've tried to do is present an introduction to the business rules approach to application development. I began by talking about the trend throughout the history of the IT field toward *raising the level of abstraction.* Raising the level of abstraction means moving toward **WHAT,** not **HOW**—telling the system what we want to do, *declaratively,* instead of how to do it, *procedurally.* This trend is desirable because declarative means the system does the work, while procedural means the user does the work.

Next, we looked at the three parts of an application—the *presentation* aspects, the *database* aspects, and the *application-specific* aspects—and we saw that the first two parts have been reasonably well automated for some time; now it's time to automate the third part, the application-specific aspects. And that's what business rules are all about, in a nutshell.

Then we took a look at the customers and orders example, assuming SQL for definiteness (as I've done all through this part of the book, of course, where it made any difference).

Next, we took a closer look at some of the ideas that were illustrated by the customers and orders example, and we saw that *the data model* is really the crucial element (it's the place to start—the rules all "hang off" the data model, in one way or another). I also gave some more searching examples, based on the suppliers and parts database: for example, the rule that suppliers S1 and S4 had to be located in the same city. We'll revisit those more searching examples in Part II.

Last, I sketched the potential advantages and disadvantages—or opportunities ("future requirements"), rather—of the business rules approach.

I'll end with a few final remarks (three of them, to be precise).

First—I didn't really call out the point explicitly before, but you might very well have realized the fact for yourself—what we're really doing with the business rules approach is not so much developing individual applications as such. Rather, we're developing *entire integrated application systems* (entire application "suites," as we used to call them). What's more, those integrated systems might possibly be more than just application systems as such; rather, they might be entire *database* systems (since database definition might very well be done via the rule engine as well, possibly iteratively, possibly interleaved with development of applications). Indeed, let me now admit that my overall title for this book is really not very good . . . I describe it as addressing the business rules approach to application development, but perhaps it would be better to talk in terms of the business rules approach to *system* development instead. In particular, of course, the data model and the database don't just serve one application, they serve whole suites of applications (whole application systems, in other words).

As an aside, I'd like to suggest too that the term "application development" is not very good either, because historically, at least, it has always meant that somebody, somewhere, is writing procedural code. And, of course, the whole point of the business rules approach is that we want to get away from writing code! In a sense, therefore, we don't really want to be "developing applications" *at all*, at least insofar as that term is traditionally understood. (After all, the business objective was never to *develop* applications; rather, it was to *execute* them!)

The second of my final remarks consists basically of another quote from that same interview with Val Huber that I mentioned in Chapter 1. Here Huber is making a business case, or at least the beginnings of a business case, for adopting the business rules approach. The interviewer had asked: "What advice would you give to IT professionals trying to make the case for adopting a rule-based approach?" Here's Huber's answer:

*The message*

> **I would suggest they look at the application backlog and the number of business systems that are needed but haven't been implemented because there aren't enough resources . . . I would then build my case on the loss of competitive edge associated with those delayed projects. A rule-based approach . . . would give the company the ability to implement and adapt applications more quickly, thus enabling them to adapt more quickly to changing business requirements.**
>
> **I would also suggest that they look at the new technologies that are available on the market and all the existing systems that are not able to use them because the conversion would be too costly—Internet, three-tiered architectures, and client/server, for example. Again, a rule-based [approach] provides the solution to the inertia found in the companies' legacy systems. Given the speed with which technology is changing today, every system we write will be a legacy system within three years. The ability to redeploy a system into any architecture on the basis of declarative specifications is the solution.**
>
> **—Val Huber**

I don't think these remarks need any embellishment by me.

And my third and very last "final remark"—just to say it one more time, to reinforce the message of this entire part of the book—is simply this:

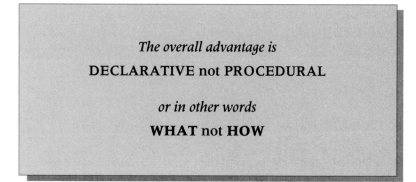

*The overall advantage is*

**DECLARATIVE not PROCEDURAL**

*or in other words*

**WHAT not HOW**

# A Relational Perspective

In this second part of the book, we'll take another look at some of the ideas presented in Part I, this time specifically from a relational point of view. As I mentioned in the preface, business rule technology is very much in the spirit of "the original relational vision," and it's interesting and instructive, and I think rather important, to see just how the two sets of ideas fit together. Indeed, much of what the business rules community is doing is implementing certain relational ideas that ought really to have been implemented in the "relational" products (or, at least, the SQL products) but—very unfortunately, in my opinion—weren't.

There are seven chapters in this part, most of them again quite short:

I assume you have a basic understanding of what the relational model is all about—although, to be frank, a large part of the material that follows consists essentially of a review of the relevant portions of the model. Indeed, we won't really get to the relevance (the obvious relevance, anyway) of relational ideas to business rule technology specifically until we reach the penultimate chapter, Chapter 14.

# Some Technical Preliminaries

## 9

As stated in the introduction to this part of the book, business rules are very much in keeping with **The Original Relational Vision.** Thus, business rules can be seen in some respects as the next (and *giant*) evolutionary step in implementing that vision. At least, such is my belief; one of the things I want to do in the chapters that follow is convince you this belief is correct.

In order to achieve this goal, however, I need to detour through a lot of relational highways and byways and lay a lot of groundwork first. Indeed, most of this part of the book is really concerned with laying that groundwork. Now, you might know some of this material already (and if so, then I apologize), but it's my experience that many people who really ought to know this material in fact don't. Not that it's at all difficult, I hasten to add—it isn't; but it *is* fundamental, and database professionals, at least, ought to be thoroughly familiar with it.

Let me get a little bit more specific. In Part I of this book, I suggested that business rules should be an integral part of the data model, not something built on top of that model, and should therefore be supported directly by the DBMS, not by some separate software component. (Let me remind you too that, as explained in Part I, when I say "data model" in contexts such as this one, I mean the term in its second sense: namely, a model of the persistent data of some particular enterprise. In this part of the book, however, I'm also going to be talking about the relational model specifically, and of course the relational model is a data model in the first sense—it's an abstract model of data in general. I hope this kind of dual usage of terminology on my part won't cause any confusion.)

Now, it's true that, as suggested in Chapter 5, implementing business rules in the DBMS instead of in a separate software component might imply a loss of independence, of a kind: It means you're dependent on the DBMS in question (at least to the extent that you're using any proprietary features of that DBMS). By contrast, implementing those rules in a separate "middleware" component means applications can be independent of the database server platform, and can perhaps even span servers, as we saw in Chapter 5. Still, never mind; let's agree to ignore that loss of independence for the time being, and let's take a closer look at the idea of incorporating business rules into the data model and see where that idea leads us. As I've already said, I need to begin by considering—or *re*considering, perhaps—some very basic aspects of the relational model.

Here then is the plan for this part of the book. Following this preliminary chapter, I'll say something about views, base tables, and stored tables (a topic about which, somewhat surprisingly, there's a lot of confusion in the IT community). Then I'll examine the crucial question of integrity constraints, and offer some observations on the relationship between integrity constraints and business rules. That discussion will pave the way for a "new" understanding of what relational databases, and relations *per se,* are really all about. After all of that groundwork, I'll be able—finally!—to show how nicely business rule technology and the relational model do indeed fit together, as claimed.

*Note:* Before I go any further, I must make it crystal clear that I'll be primarily concerned in what follows with the underlying theory, not just with commercial pragma. Theory is important! What's more, it's *practical* . . . I have a great quote in this connection:

> **Those who are enamored of practice without theory are like a pilot who goes into a ship without rudder or compass and never has any certainty where he [*sic*] is going. Practice should always be based upon a sound knowledge of theory.**
>
> **—Leonardo da Vinci (1452–1519)**

As noted in Chapter 5, the theory we're talking about here, relational theory, is very practical indeed.

To make the same point in different words: In what follows, we'll be talking about principles, not products, and foundations, not fads. Of course, I do understand that compromises and tradeoffs are sometimes necessary "in the real world" for various pragmatic reasons; however, I believe very firmly that such compromises and tradeoffs should always be made *from a position of conceptual strength*. To be specific, you should be aware that you *are* making a compromise (when you are), you should know exactly *why* (and the reason had better be a good one!), and of course you should *document* what you're doing, and why, in all such cases.

I'll be basing most of my examples in this part of the book on the well-known suppliers and parts database once again. The following figure gives a set of sample values for that database (the corresponding data definitions, consisting of three SQL CREATE TABLE statements, were shown in outline in Chapter 4). Just to remind you:

| S | S# | SNAME | STATUS | CITY |
|---|----|-------|--------|------|
|   | S1 | Smith | 20 | London |
|   | S2 | Jones | 10 | Paris |
|   | S3 | Blake | 30 | Paris |
|   | S4 | Clark | 20 | London |
|   | S5 | Adams | 30 | Athens |

| SP | S# | P# | QTY |
|----|----|----|-----|
|    | S1 | P1 | 300 |
|    | S1 | P2 | 200 |
|    | S1 | P3 | 400 |
|    | S1 | P4 | 200 |
|    | S1 | P5 | 100 |
|    | S1 | P6 | 100 |
|    | S2 | P1 | 300 |
|    | S2 | P2 | 400 |
|    | S3 | P2 | 200 |
|    | S4 | P2 | 200 |
|    | S4 | P4 | 300 |
|    | S4 | P5 | 400 |

| P | P# | PNAME | COLOR | WEIGHT | CITY |
|---|----|-------|-------|--------|------|
|   | P1 | Nut | Red | 12 | London |
|   | P2 | Bolt | Green | 17 | Paris |
|   | P3 | Screw | Blue | 17 | Rome |
|   | P4 | Screw | Red | 14 | London |
|   | P5 | Cam | Blue | 12 | Paris |
|   | P6 | Cog | Red | 19 | London |

■ There's a suppliers table S, with supplier number {S#} as primary key and some other items (supplier name, status, and city or location);

■ There's a parts table P, with part number {P#} as primary key and some other items (part name, color, weight, and city or location);

■ And there's a shipments table SP, showing which suppliers are shipping, or supplying, which parts in which quantities. The primary key for shipments is the combination {S#,P#} of supplier number and part number (and {S#} and {P#} are foreign keys, of course, referring to suppliers and parts, respectively).

Now, here comes a *very* important preliminary: *the distinction between **values** and **variables.** This distinction is absolutely fundamental! It's also very obvious—we've certainly known about it, and understood it, ever since programming languages first appeared on the scene, and probably before that—but people do get confused over it surprisingly often. (In fairness, I should say that in fact it's all too easy to make mistakes in this connection, as we'll see in just a moment.)

Anyway, first let me pin the difference down. Here are some definitions, taken from a book by J. Craig Cleaveland [3]:

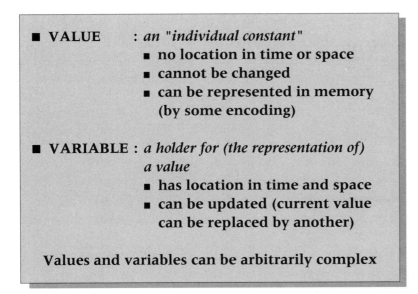

- **VALUE** : *an "individual constant"*
  - **no location in time or space**
  - **cannot be changed**
  - **can be represented in memory (by some encoding)**

- **VARIABLE** : *a holder for (the representation of) a value*
  - **has location in time and space**
  - **can be updated (current value can be replaced by another)**

**Values and variables can be arbitrarily complex**

To elaborate:

- First, a **value** is an *"individual constant,"* like the integer 3 or the character string 'Joe'. As Cleaveland puts it, values *have no location in time or space*. They simply *exist*. For example, there's just one integer 3 "in the universe" (as it were), and it's available for use by anybody who wants to use it for any purpose. So if we want to say that (for example) employee Joe has three dependents, we can use the integer 3 to do that. How? Well, although the integer 3 as such "has no location in time or space," it can be *represented in memory* (by some encoding), and of course such representations in memory certainly do have locations in time and space. So we can put a *copy*, or *appearance*, of the integer 3—or, rather, a copy or appearance of *some encoding of* the integer 3—in some variable that denotes the number of Joe's dependents. And, of course, we can also put a copy or appearance of that same integer 3 in other variables too, to denote (say) the number of hours worked on some project, or the number of days remaining before some deadline, or any number of other things besides.

*Very important:* Note that, by definition, the one thing we can't do to any value is change or update it! Because, of course, if we could update (say) the integer 3, then after the update it wouldn't be that integer any more.

■ Second, a **variable** is, of course, *a holder or container for an appearance of a value* (more precisely, a container for an appearance of some encoding of a value). And (also of course) variables do have locations in time and space. What's more, variables, unlike values, can be updated (meaning the current value of the variable can be replaced by another value, probably different).

By the way, it's important to understand that (as the figure indicates) values and variables can be arbitrarily complex. We're not limited to simple things like the integer 3. For example, we can have color values, ellipse values, circle values, fingerprint values, polygon values, X-ray values (and on and on). It follows that we can also have color variables, ellipse variables, circle variables (and on and on).

So much for values *vs.* variables. I hope you agree the distinction is quite straightforward; yet, as I've already indicated, it seems to be all too easy to fall into traps in this area. In particular, the object world seems to fall into such traps with great frequency. Here's an example, taken from a tutorial on object databases [29] (the interspersed remarks in italics are mine):

> We distinguish the declared type of a variable from . . . the type of the object that is the current value of the variable [*so an object is a value*] . . . we distinguish objects from values [*so an object isn't a value after all*] . . . a **mutator** [is an operator such that it's] possible to observe its effect on some object [*so a mutator is something that updates an object, and hence in fact an object is a variable —since, as we've already seen, it's precisely* **variables** *that are updatable, by definition*].

So what exactly is an object? Is it a value? Is it a variable? Is it both? Is it something else entirely?

Now I want to turn to the relational world. Sad to say, there's been some confusion over the values *vs.* variables distinction in the relational world as well—specifically, over the distinction between *relation* values and variables. First, a **relation value** is just a relation *per se* (in exactly the same way that an integer value is just an integer *per se*). The figure earlier in this chapter that gave some sample values for the suppliers and parts database shows three such relation values—ones that happen to exist in that particular database at some particular time. More precisely, those three relation values are the ones that happen to be the values at that particular time of three particular **relation variables** (and, of course, the relation variables in question are called S, P, and SP, respectively).

Let's look at an analogy. Suppose we say in some programming language:

```
DECLARE N INTEGER ... ;
```

N here isn't an integer *per se*, it's an integer *variable* whose *values* are integers *per se*—different integers at different times (after all, that's basically what variable means). And we all understand this point. Well, in exactly the same way, if we say in SQL:

```
CREATE TABLE T ... ;
```

T here isn't a table *per se,* it's a table *variable* whose *values* are tables *per se*—different tables at different times. Well, actually I'd like to begin talking in terms of *relations* rather than *tables* (at least some of the time), so let me rephrase the foregoing: T here isn't a relation *per se,* it's a relation *variable* whose *values* are relations *per se*—different relations at different times.

The following figure illustrates the distinction between relation values and relation variables.

*Relation values* vs. *relation variables*

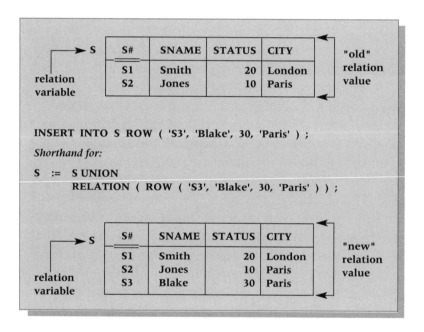

In general, when we "update T" (for example, by "inserting a row" into T—T here being the relation variable we defined by means of that statement "CREATE TABLE T" a few moments ago), what we're really doing is *replacing the old relation value of T en bloc by a new, different relation value.* Of course, it's true that the old value and the new value are somewhat similar—the new one just has one more row than the old one—but conceptually they *are* different values.

Let's take a closer look at the example in the figure. We start off with a relation variable called S containing two supplier rows—its current value is a relation with two rows of data. Then we "insert a third row." What that INSERT really is, however, is shorthand for a certain **relational assignment.**\* Like all assignments, that assignment works by evaluating the expression on the right-hand side and then assigning the result of that evaluation to the variable on the left-hand side. In the example, therefore, we first form the union of "S" (meaning the current two-row value of the relation variable S) and a relation containing just the row we want to insert. That gives us a new relation—a new relation *value*—with three rows. Then we assign that new relation value to the relation variable S, thereby achieving the desired overall result.

So you can see that, logically speaking, INSERT is really just shorthand for a certain relational assignment. And the same is true of DELETE too, of course, and also UPDATE: In all three cases, we're really just talking about (useful!) shorthands. Thus, the *fundamental* update operator—indeed, the only one we really need, speaking from a purely logical point of view—is relational assignment.

Furthermore, it should be clear by now that *relation value* and *relation variable* really are two very different concepts. The trouble is, historically we've tended to use just the one term, "relation," for both; we've tended to talk about just "relations" and mean sometimes relation values and sometimes relation variables. And—regrettably—this fact has certainly led to some confusion in the past (in the realm of normalization, for example).

Now, you might possibly be aware that, along with my colleague Hugh Darwen, I've been at work for several years

---

\*The relational assignment shown in the figure is not a valid SQL statement (indeed, SQL doesn't directly support relational assignment at all!). The INSERT statement is also not valid SQL (SQL would require the keyword ROW to be replaced by the keyword VALUES).

on something called *The Third Manifesto* [9] (I mentioned this work in passing in Chapter 7). *The Third Manifesto* is a detailed proposal for the future of data and database systems. And, given the confusions I've just mentioned, we decided in our *Manifesto* to introduce the term **relvar** as a convenient shorthand for "relation variable." Thus, a relation variable or "relvar" is a named variable whose permitted values are relation values. And then we framed our remarks throughout the *Manifesto* in terms of relation variables or relvars when it was really relation variables that we meant, and in terms of relation values, or just relations for short, when it was really relation values that we meant. And I would frankly prefer to do the same thing in the rest of this book . . . However, I didn't want to load up the text with too many new terms as well as (possibly) new concepts, and I felt that using the term *relvar* might get in the way of the real message I wanted to get across. So I decided, a little reluctantly, to stay with the term *relation* (or even *table,* sometimes), for reasons of familiarity. But it's worth keeping the relation *vs.* relvar distinction in mind!—it's very important as an aid to precise thinking, and it can help avoid confusion. I will at least remind you of the distinction from time to time in the chapters that follow, even though (as I say) I won't try to use the terminology systematically myself.

# Views,
# Base Tables, and
# Stored Tables

## 10

As its title indicates, this chapter is concerned with views *vs.* base tables *vs.* stored tables, or what might more accurately be characterized in *Third Manifesto* terms as "virtual relvars *vs.* base relvars *vs.* stored relvars"—views being, in effect, *virtual tables,* and tables in this context being relation variables.* As I noted in Chapter 9, there's a surprising amount of confusion out in the industry on this topic, too.

First of all, it's in the fundamental nature of the relational model that it's concerned with logical issues, not physical ones. It deliberately has absolutely nothing whatsoever to say regarding physical (that is, implementation) issues. In particular, therefore, base tables—which are certainly a feature of the relational model—are a logical concept, not a physical one. Yet just about every SQL product on the market, so far as I know, treats base tables as a very physical kind of thing . . . Certainly those products all map base tables to stored tables in a very direct, almost one-to-one kind of way, and stored tables are definitely physical constructs (and hence an implementation issue, not a model one). In my opinion, this state of affairs represents a serious defect in those products.

---

*Actually, base relvars are called *real* relvars in *The Third Manifesto,* precisely because (in contrast to views) they're real, not virtual.

To repeat, the relational model does have something to say about base tables—and also about views, of course, which are virtual tables that are defined on top of those base tables—but it has nothing to say (nothing direct, at any rate) about stored tables as such. The following figure illustrates the situation.

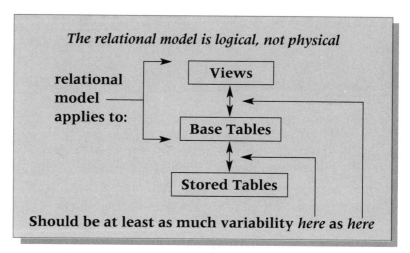

The point of the figure is as follows. First, of course, "everyone knows" that views are a logical concept, and there can be an arbitrary degree of variability between views and base tables (views can be joins, projections, unions, and so on, of base tables). Well, base tables are a logical concept too, and there should be at least as much variability possible between base tables and stored tables as there is between views and base tables! Thus, base tables should be allowed to be joins, projections, unions, and so on, of stored tables. Why ever not?

By the way, note that to say that base tables can be joins, projections, unions, and so on, of stored tables is to imply the converse as well—namely, that stored tables can be joins, projections, unions, and so on, of base tables. For example, if base table T is the join of stored tables T1 and T2, then stored tables T1 and T2 are projections of base table T. Likewise, if base tables T1 and T2 are (judiciously chosen) projections of stored table T, then stored table T is the join of base tables T1 and T2.

To say it again, then, base tables should not necessarily map one-to-one to stored tables. The only real requirement is that it must be possible to obtain the base tables from the stored tables somehow—because, of course, if we can obtain the base tables, then we can obtain everything else. Thus, a stored table should be allowed to be **any expressible table** (not necessarily a base table) that can be supported in some "direct, efficient" manner—where:

- By *expressible,* I mean the stored table in question can be obtained from the given base tables by means of some expression of the relational algebra (thus, "expressible tables" include all base tables and all derived tables).

- By *direct* and *efficient,* I mean, basically, that indexes or other physical access paths will exist on the disk to facilitate fast access to the stored table in question.

In other words, we should be able to store joins, restrictions, projections, unions, summaries, and so on—possibly even with some degree of *controlled redundancy,* by which I mean that it might even be possible (a) to store the "same" data several times in several different ways, in order to support several different kinds of queries on that data with equal efficiency, and (b) have the system manage that redundancy and hide it from the user.

*Note:* Some of today's SQL products do support the foregoing ideas to some limited extent. For example, some products let you store the rows from two base tables interleaved on the disk, thereby effectively storing a join of the two base tables as a single stored table; and if the user now asks to join the two base tables in question, well, that join will be very fast. Other products let you store "partitions" (disjoint restrictions) of a single base table as separate stored tables. And in some of the more recent *data warehouse* products, you can even store summaries—precomputed aggregate values—transparently, in the sense that the user isn't aware that those summaries are indeed stored (an example of the "controlled redundancy" notion mentioned in the previous paragraph). But by and large the support for such variability tends to be fairly meager, so far as I'm aware.

From all of the above, it follows that base tables are (or should be) truly a logical concept, not a physical one;

they are (or should be) no more physical than views are. In fact, base tables and views are often logically interchangeable! To say the same thing in different words, *the choice as to which tables are base tables and which views is often fairly arbitrary.* (To examine this important issue in depth would take us much too far afield here, unfortunately; see reference [7] for a detailed discussion.)

It further follows that the base tables in a given database should reflect a clean logical design for that database, with absolutely no entanglement whatsoever with physical or performance matters. The SQL vendors really let us down here! As I've already said, base tables today do tend to be rather close to physical storage . . . whence the massive confusion over *denormalization,* of course. To elaborate:

- As soon as SQL products first began to appear, the cry went up that you had to "denormalize for performance." I'm sure you've heard this claim—people are still making it to this very day.

- And, of course, it's true that denormalization for performance reasons is sometimes necessary.

- However, any necessary denormalization clearly ought to be done at the physical storage level, not at the logical (base table) level. Because most SQL systems today essentially equate these two levels, however, there has been, and continues to be, much confusion over this simple point.

- And because of the lack of a clean separation between the two levels, denormalization usually has the effect of corrupting an otherwise clean logical design, with well-known undesirable consequences. (Every time we've done this kind of thing in the past, we've paid for it in the long run.)

Now I'd like to say a few words regarding views. The first point I need to make is that a brand new confusion factor seems to be being introduced, almost as we speak, in connection with this topic! I refer to the deprecated term "materialized view," which is often used (especially in data warehouse contexts) to mean something that's not a view at all, but rather what has historically—and certainly much preferably—been called a *snapshot*.* A snapshot is a base table (probably one that does, for performance reasons, map one-to-one to a stored table) whose values are derived in some way from other tables. Such a table does resemble a view insofar as its values are, as just stated, derived from other tables; however, it differs in that it's real, not virtual—meaning it's represented not just by its definition in terms of other tables, but also (at least conceptually) by its own separate copy of the data. To call a snapshot "a materialized view" is to muddle some very fundamental issues! While it's true that certain products do sometimes "materialize views" for performance or other reasons, such materialization is an implementation issue entirely; views by definition are *never* "materialized" as far as the user is concerned. From the perspective of the relational model, in other words, views simply are *not* "materialized," and a "materialized view" is a contradiction in terms.

In sharp contrast to the foregoing, the term *view* in this book is (of course) used to mean a view in the conventional relational model sense.

With that little digression out of the way, let me now repeat something I said at the beginning of this chapter: namely, that views are *virtual relation variables.* Note in particular, therefore, that they are indeed *variables*—implying, therefore, that views, just like base tables, are or should be updatable too. This is another place where the SQL vendors really let us down . . . View updating is notoriously weak in SQL products today. Though here I should add, in fairness, that the vendors do have some excuse for this one, because the theory of view updating wasn't worked out until comparatively recently. However, it has been worked out

---

*For example, the following are all titles of papers from the 1997 ACM SIGMOD International Conference on Management of Data (Tucson, Ariz., May 1997): "Efficient View Maintenance at Data Warehouses"; "On-Line Warehouse View Maintenance"; "Supporting Multiple View Maintenance Policies." In all of these papers, the "views" referred to in the title are not views at all but snapshots.

now [10]. This isn't the place to get into specifics; let me just say that it's now been shown that, contrary to conventional wisdom, views are *always* updatable, logically speaking. (At least in principle. Of course, a view update will fail if it violates an integrity constraint, but that's true of all updating, for base tables as well as views.) So join views are updatable, union views are updatable, difference views are updatable (and so on).

It's relevant to mention here too that when you're doing logical database design, some entity types more properly map to views rather than to base tables. We don't need to get into too much detail on this issue either; there's just one point I want to make. To be specific:

■ The new SQL standard SQL:1999 (previously known as "SQL3") includes a very weird notion it calls "subtables and supertables" [16].

■ And in my opinion that notion should never have made it into the standard at all—because in fact views solve the problem that "subtables and supertables" are supposed to solve, and they do it better, too. What's more, they do it without introducing any new concepts; in other words, the relational model already had the necessary capabilities to solve the problem in question.

However, it's true that the view solution does rely on recognizing that, to repeat, some entity types map to views rather than base tables [7,9].

My final point is this: As far as the user is concerned, views are (or should be) indistinguishable from base tables! To the user, views *are* base tables. For example, suppose I'm the DBA and you're a user. Then I might define a certain view V and give it to you to use. But you don't know it's a view!—I do, but you don't. As far as you're concerned, table V is a base table, and it must look and feel just like a base table: It must have *all* and *only* the properties of base tables (like keys and so forth). In particular, it *must* be updatable!— and view updatability is thus *a hard requirement.* I'll have more to say on this important point in Chapter 13.

# Integrity Constraints

# 11

❖ ❖ ❖

Recall from Chapter 4 that an integrity constraint is, in essence, a conditional expression that must evaluate to *true*. Here's an example from the customers and orders database:

```
TOTAL_OWED ≤ CREDIT_LIMIT
```

If an update is attempted that would make this expression *false*, the update is rejected, and an error message is sent back to the user.

It should be clear that integrity constraints are crucially important, since they control the correctness of the data. In many ways, in fact, integrity constraints are **the** most important part of the system. In particular, they're much more important than *performance* (it doesn't matter at all how fast your queries run if you can't trust the answers you get to be correct). *Note:* I suppose I should admit that not everybody agrees with me on this question, but I stand by my position, and I'm prepared to defend it if necessary!

Now, I'm sure you've realized already that what the database world calls (and has been calling for many, many years) integrity constraints is largely just business rules by another name. But this part of the book is really about databases (for the most part, at any rate), so I'm going to stay with the term *integrity constraints* for the time being.

What I want to do in this chapter, then, is present a taxonomy or classification scheme for integrity constraints. The scheme I'm going to describe is the one I had in mind when I said in Part I of this book, in Chapter 4, that I'd be discussing a much more precise and more useful taxonomy than the one we looked at in Part I (the one from the book by Odell [19], if you recall). Now, over the years, many such taxonomies have been proposed, by many different people, but I'm going to stick my neck out here and suggest that—at last—we have one that's *correct*.

You probably won't be surprised to learn that the scheme I'm going to describe is the one advocated in *The Third Manifesto* [9]. And the reason I think it's correct is because the structure of the scheme mirrors the structure of the data itself. For consider: The database is made out of tables; tables are made out of columns; and columns are made out of domains. So we have *database* constraints, at the overall database level; *table* constraints, at the individual table level; *column* constraints, at the individual column level; and *domain* constraints, at the individual domain level. To be more specific:

■ *Domain constraints* specify the legal values for a given domain. *Note:* Actually, it's one of the fundamental tenets of *The Third Manifesto* that what the relational community calls a domain is nothing more nor less than what the programming languages community calls a *data type* (*type* for short). For a variety of reasons, in fact, we really prefer the term *type;* however, we do use *domain* as well, treating the two terms as interchangeable, and I'll do the same in this book. Thus, domain constraints are often referred to as *type* constraints in what follows.

  By the way, it's important to understand that the types or domains in question can be either system-defined types (typically rather simple ones—for example, integers, character strings) or user-defined types, of arbitrary complexity (for example, geometric points, ellipses, polygons). As I said in Chapter 9, we're not limited to simple things like integers and strings.

- *Column constraints* specify the legal values for a given column (or *attribute,* to use the more formal term—but I'll stick to *column*).

- *Table constraints* specify the legal values for a given table (more precisely, a given *relvar*). *Note:* Table constraints can also be *transition* constraints. Recall from Chapter 4 that a transition constraint specifies legal transitions from one value to another—for example, "salaries can never decrease." For simplicity, however, I'll ignore transition constraints in what follows, except for a couple of examples near the end of the chapter.

- *Database constraints* specify the legal values for a given database. Again they might be transition constraints, in general, but, to repeat, I'm mostly going to ignore transition constraints.

This taxonomy is summarized below.

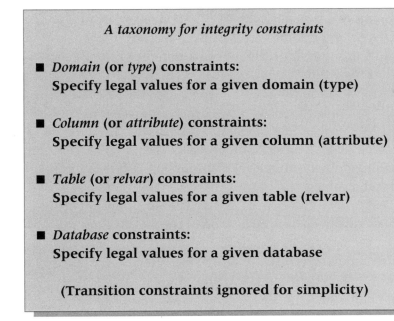

A taxonomy for integrity constraints

- **Domain (or *type*) constraints:**
  **Specify legal values for a given domain (type)**

- **Column (or *attribute*) constraints:**
  **Specify legal values for a given column (attribute)**

- **Table (or *relvar*) constraints:**
  **Specify legal values for a given table (relvar)**

- **Database constraints:**
  **Specify legal values for a given database**

  **(Transition constraints ignored for simplicity)**

*A taxonomy for integrity constraints*

Let's look at some examples. *Note:* The examples that follow are deliberately not expressed in SQL; rather, they're expressed in a relational language called **Tutorial D,** defined in reference [9] and used there as a vehicle for explaining the concepts of *The Third Manifesto*. I'll use **Tutorial D** as a basis for examples throughout the remainder of this part of the book, explaining whatever aspects of the language seem to need such explanation as we go.

Here then are some examples of **type** (or domain) **constraints,** all of them involving user-defined types:

```
TYPE QTY
    POSSREP { Q INTEGER WHERE Q > 0 AND Q < 5001 } ;
```

This first example defines a type or domain called QTY ("quantity"), with a **possible representation** ("POSSREP") consisting of an integer called Q. What this means is that it must at least be possible to represent quantities by means of integers; it doesn't mean that quantities are actually represented as integers—they might be, or they might be represented as floating point numbers, or character strings, or anything else you can think of. *Note:* This POSSREP notion is one that pervades *The Third Manifesto*. It turns out to be very important, for all kinds of reasons; however, those reasons aren't really of concern to us here, so I won't bother to go into details.

Anyway, you can see that we've used the POSSREP in the example to specify a type constraint (see the WHERE clause): Quantities must be such that they can be represented by, precisely, the integers 1, 2, . . . , 5000— meaning (loosely) that legal quantities are just those five thousand values.

As this first example suggests, type constraints in general are essentially just a specification of the set of values that make up the type in question; in effect, they're just an enumeration of that set of legal values. Here's an example in which the constraint is actually expressed as such an enumeration:

```
TYPE COLOR
    POSSREP { C CHAR WHERE
                C IN { 'Red', 'Yellow', 'Blue', 'Green' } }
```

Legal colors are red, yellow, blue, and green.

And one further example of a type constraint:

```
TYPE ELLIPSE
    POSSREP { A LENGTH, B LENGTH, CTR POINT WHERE A ≥ B } ;
```

Ellipses can possibly be represented by their major semiaxis *a*, their minor semiaxis *b*, and their center *ctr*. The semiaxes are lengths and the center is a point (LENGTH and POINT are further user-defined types, whose definitions aren't shown). The ELLIPSE type constraint specifies that the major semiaxis *a* must be greater than or equal to the minor semiaxis *b*.

While we're on the subject of type constraints, by the way, I should mention that **"IS A"** constraints are an important special case. For example:

```
TYPE CIRCLE IS ELLIPSE WHERE
        THE_A ( ELLIPSE ) = THE_B ( ELLIPSE )
        POSSREP { R   = THE_A   ( ELLIPSE ) ,
                  CTR = THE_CTR ( ELLIPSE ) } ;
```

The specification CIRCLE IS ELLIPSE is part of the type constraint. It means that every circle "IS A" ellipse, and type CIRCLE is a *subtype* of *supertype* ELLIPSE. Type CIRCLE thus "inherits" various properties from type ELLIPSE—for example, the property of having an area (circles have an area, because all ellipses have an area). However, circles also have certain properties of their own that ellipses in general don't have (for example, circles have a radius, but ellipses in general don't).

Incidentally, note the additional specification (also part of the type constraint):

```
THE_A ( ELLIPSE ) = THE_B ( ELLIPSE )
```

This specification indicates that a circle is precisely an ellipse for which the semiaxes *a* and *b* are equal. (The operators THE_A and THE_B should be self-explanatory.)

Finally, note that circles have a "POSSREP" consisting of a radius R and a center CTR, defined to be equal to the major semiaxis and the center, respectively, of the particular ellipse that the circle in question happens to be.

(As an aside, I'd like to say that *The Third Manifesto* includes extensive support for the whole business of subtyping and inheritance in general, including support for both *single* and *multiple* inheritance and support for *scalar, row,* and *table* type inheritance. The details are, obviously, far beyond the scope of this book; all I wanted to do here was point out the relevance of type constraints to that support. Reference [9] gives full details, of course.)

Now let's turn to **column constraints.** Like domain (or type) constraints, column constraints are also fairly simple; the column constraint for some given column *C* is essentially just a statement to the effect that values of that column are drawn from some given domain or type *D*. Here are some examples—to be specific, the column constraints for the columns of the suppliers table S:

```
S.S#      IN S#
S.SNAME   IN NAME
S.STATUS  IN INTEGER
S.CITY    IN CHAR
```

The symbol "S" in these constraints denotes an arbitrary suppliers row. For simplicity (though perhaps a little unrealistically), I'm assuming that columns STATUS and CITY are defined on some simple system-defined types (INTEGER and CHAR, respectively), instead of on user-defined types as the other two columns are. Note that I'm using "S#" as the name of a domain as well as the name of a column.

Column constraints are effectively checked "immediately," or in other words at the end of each update statement, loosely speaking. For example, whenever the user tries to place a value somewhere in column SNAME (say), the system immediately checks to see whether that value is a legal NAME value; if it isn't, the statement is rejected, and no update is done.

By the way, note that column constraints don't apply just to columns in base tables!—because (as we saw in Chapter 10) it must be possible to update views as well as base tables.

Now we come to **table constraints.** A table constraint can be as complicated as you like, provided only that it refers just to the individual table in question and no others. Here's an example:

```
S.STATUS ≥ 0 AND S.STATUS ≤ 100
```

("table S can never have a value in which some row has a status value that's outside the range 0 to 100 inclusive"; note that this constraint is certainly satisfied by the sample data values shown in Chapter 9). Note too that the constraint certainly does refer to just the relevant table (namely, table S). Note finally that it can be regarded as shorthand for a more formal version that looks something like this:

```
FORALL s# IN S#, sn IN NAME, st IN INTEGER, sc IN CHAR
  ( IF { S# s#, SNAME sn, STATUS st, CITY sc } IN S
    THEN st ≥ 0 AND st ≤ 100 )
```

("for all S# values *s#*, all NAME values *sn*, all INTEGER values *st*, and all CHAR values *sc*, if a row with S# component *s#*, SNAME component *sn*, STATUS component *st*, and CITY component *sc* appears in table S, then *st* must be in the range 0 to 100 inclusive"). For obvious reasons, I'm not going to worry too much about such more formal expressions in this book; I merely remark that we'd have to worry about them if we were trying to develop this theory formally (which isn't what I'm trying to do here, of course).

By the way, please understand that the example is indeed an example of a table constraint, not a column constraint, even though it mentions just one column. Column constraints, to repeat, are constraints of the form "column *C* takes its values from domain *D*." The example is also, obviously, not a domain constraint either (domain constraints have to do with the legal values in a domain, not in a column or a table).

*Note:* Like column constraints, table constraints don't apply just to base tables, because (to say it again) we must be able to update views as well as base tables.

Here's another example of a table constraint:

```
IF S.CITY = 'London' THEN S.STATUS = 20
```

("suppliers in London must have status 20"; note again that this constraint is satisfied by the sample values shown in Chapter 9). This example refers to two distinct columns (in the same table, of course).

And one more example:

```
IF SX.S# = SY.S# THEN SX.SNAME  = SY.SNAME
                 AND  SX.STATUS = SY.STATUS
                 AND  SX.CITY   = SY.CITY
```

("if supplier rows SX and SY have the same supplier number, then they also have the same name, status, and city; hence they're really the same row, and {S#} is a *superkey*"). *Note:* In case you're not familiar with the term "superkey," let me explain:

- First, a *candidate* key is a set of columns that can serve as a unique identifier for the table in question and includes no column that's unnecessary for unique identification purposes. For example, {S#} is a candidate key for suppliers, but {S#,CITY} isn't (because of the CITY column, which isn't needed to identify suppliers).

- Second, a *superkey* is a superset of a candidate key (so a candidate key is always a superkey, but the converse is false). For example, {S#,CITY} is a superkey for suppliers. So is {S#}, of course.

- Finally, a *primary* key is a candidate key that's chosen for some reason to be "more equal than the others." (If indeed there are any others, that is. If there's just one candidate key, no harm is done by calling it primary. But if there are two or more, then which if any is to be regarded as primary is essentially a matter of psychology, not logic, and I certainly don't want to get into that kind of issue here.)

Like column constraints, table constraints are checked immediately (where, to say it again, "immediately" means at the end of each update statement, loosely speaking). Thus, whenever the user tries to update table S, for example, the system immediately checks to see whether the new table value is a legal value for S; if it isn't, the statement is rejected, and no update is done.

Last of all, we have **database constraints.** Like table constraints, a database constraint can be as complicated as you like, provided only that it refers to at least two distinct tables (it must be at least two, because otherwise the constraint isn't a database constraint after all but a table constraint). Here's an example (repeated from Chapter 6):

```
IF S.STATUS < 20 AND S.S# = SP.S# THEN SP.QTY ≤ QTY(500)
```

("suppliers with status less than 20 must not supply any part in a quantity greater than 500"; note the QTY literal, QTY(500), and note too that—yet again—this constraint is satisfied by the sample data values shown in Chapter 9). Note that the constraint certainly does refer to two tables, S and SP (note in particular the "join term" that interrelates them). Note too that the constraint can be regarded as shorthand for a more formal version that looks something like this:

```
FORALL s# IN S#, sn IN NAME, st IN INTEGER, sc IN CHAR,
       p# IN P#, q IN INTEGER
  ( IF { S# s#, SNAME sn, STATUS st, CITY sc } IN S
    AND { S# s#, P# p#, QTY q } IN SP AND st < 20
    THEN q ≤ QTY(500) )
```

Again, however, I'm not going to worry too much about such more formal expressions here.

A couple of points arising from this example:

- First, observe that we distinguish between single- and multi-*table* constraints, not between single- and multi-*row* constraints. For example, the superkey constraint shown earlier for table S is certainly a single-table constraint, even though it talks about two rows (SX and SY). In the past, by contrast, taxonomies for integrity constraints have typically drawn a dividing line between single- and multi-*row* constraints; however, that distinction, it seems to me, is one that's more important from an implementation point of view than it is from a logical one.

- Second, database constraints, like column and table constraints, are checked immediately—another point of difference between the taxonomy under discussion and others in the past. In previous schemes, multi-table constraints, at least (and possibly others too), were checked at COMMIT time (that is, at end-of-transaction) instead of immediately. In particular, the SQL standard [16] includes something it calls "DEFERRED checking" (though in SQL the checking is done at COMMIT time *at the latest*—it might actually be done *before* end-of-transaction—but that's a detail we can ignore here). Deferred checking leads to major problems, however, of both a theoretical and a practical nature; in *The Third Manifesto,* therefore, we take the position that *all* checking must be immediate.*

Here are a couple more examples of database constraints:

```
EXISTS S ( S.S# = SP.S# )
```

This example defines the foreign key constraint from shipments to suppliers ("for every shipment SP, there must exist a supplier S with the same supplier number"; note the use of the existential quantifier, EXISTS). Note that the constraint is indeed a database constraint, because it spans two tables.

```
EXISTS P ( P.P# = SP.P# )
```

This example is similar to the previous one.

Some pragmatically important special cases arise in connection with database constraints. For example, consider the notions of *kernel, characteristic,* and *associative entities,* which are intuitively useful concepts in connection with

---

*It's true that certain constraints (especially database ones) involve keeping distinct data items "in synch," as it were, and hence that certain data items sometimes need to be updated at the same time, in effect. *The Third Manifesto* provides a parallel form of assignment in order to take care of this requirement.

logical database design. (The terms are taken from Codd's extended relational model RM/T [5,6].) Briefly:

- A **kernel** entity is one that has independent existence (kernels are "what the database is really all about"— they're the entry points into the database, in effect). In our running example, suppliers and parts are kernels.

- A **characteristic** entity is one that further describes or "characterizes" some other entity (and is existence-dependent on that other entity). There aren't any characteristics in the suppliers and parts database, but order line items might provide an example in the customers and orders database (order line items are certainly existence-dependent on the relevant order).

- An **associative** entity is a many-to-many (or many-to-many-to-many . . .) relationship that serves to link other entities together, logically speaking. (Relationships are entities, of course!) Shipments provide an example in the suppliers and parts database.

Kernel entity types are represented by base tables (typically; sometimes they're represented by views instead, but I don't want to get into details of that possibility right now). The same is true of characteristic and associative entity types as well, of course, but the tables corresponding to such entity types have foreign keys to represent the characteristic or associative relationship. So it is indeed the case that database constraints are relevant here.

The other pragmatically important case I want to mention in connection with database constraints is **"HAS A"** (not "IS A"!) relationships. For example, a part-time employee "has a" hourly wage instead of a monthly salary. So, first, there'll be a table for employees in general, with common information such as employee number, department number, and so forth; second, there'll be a table for part-time employees specifically, giving information specific to part-time employees (for example, hourly wage); and third, there'll be a foreign key constraint—a database constraint, in fact—from the part-time employees table to the "employees in general" table.

*Note:* There's a great deal of confusion in the industry over IS A *vs.* HAS A. IS A is subtyping and inheritance and we've already talked about it briefly ("a circle IS A ellipse"). HAS A is quite different!—in particular, it isn't subtyping, and it isn't inheritance. See reference [9] if you want to investigate this distinction in depth; here I just want to make it clear that both IS A and HAS A relationships can be handled straight-forwardly within the constraint taxonomy under discussion.

Let me close this chapter by repeating the list of constraints from Chapter 4 for the suppliers and parts database and showing how they would look under the scheme I've been describing. They're the ones I said you might want to try out on your own system (assuming you have access to a system, of course). Here they are. Note that the sample values given in Chapter 9 don't violate any of them!—with the sole exception of the one about supplier and part cities being disjoint.

- Legal supplier numbers are of the form S*nnnn* (*nnnn* = up to four decimal digits).

```
TYPE S#
    POSSREP { X CHAR WHERE
              SUBSTR ( X, 1, 1 ) = 'S' AND
              IS_INTEGER ( SUBSTR ( X, 2 ) ) AND
              CHAR_LENGTH ( X ) ≤ 5 } ;
```

This first one is a domain or type constraint. I've assumed the availability of certain operators for use in expressing that constraint: SUBSTR, for extracting a substring of a given string; IS_INTEGER, for testing whether a given string denotes an integer; and CHAR_LENGTH, for obtaining the length of a given string.

- Red parts weigh less than 50 pounds.

```
IF P.COLOR = COLOR ( 'Red' )
THEN P.WEIGHT < WEIGHT ( 50 )
```

This one is a table constraint—actually a "single-row" constraint. Note the COLOR and WEIGHT literals.

- Suppliers S1 and S4 are always in the same city.

```
IF SX.S# = S# ( 'S1' ) AND SY.S# = S# ( 'S4' )
THEN SX.CITY = SY.CITY
```

This example is also a table constraint, but a "multi-row" one.

- No shipment quantity can be greater than twice the average of all such quantities.

```
SPX.QTY ≤ 2 * AVG ( SPY, QTY )
```

Another multi-row table constraint, this one involving aggregates. The expression AVG(SPY,QTY) returns the average of the values currently appearing in the QTY column of the SP table.

- Every London supplier supplies part P2.

```
IF S.CITY = 'London' THEN EXISTS ( SP WHERE SP.S# = S.S#
                                    AND SP.P# = P# ( 'P2' ) )
```

This one is a database constraint, involving exactly two tables, S and SP.

- Suppliers in Athens can move only to London or Paris.

```
IF S'.CITY = 'Athens' THEN S.CITY = 'Athens'
                      OR S.CITY = 'London'
                      OR S.CITY = 'Paris'
```

This one needs a little more explanation. First of all, note that it's a *transition* constraint (a table transition constraint, to be precise); all prior examples have been examples of state constraints instead. The primed table name S' refers to the value of table S before the update, the unprimed name S refers to the value after the update. The constraint can thus be read as follows: "If the supplier city was Athens before the update, then after the update it must be London or Paris" (unless it hasn't changed at all, in which case it's still Athens, of course).

- Supplier cities and part cities are disjoint.

```
FORALL S ( NOT EXISTS P ( P.CITY = S.CITY ) )
```

(in very stilted English, "for all suppliers, there doesn't exist a part with the same city")—another database constraint.

■ Average shipment quantities never decrease.

*No solution provided.*

This is a transition constraint involving aggregates (though only one table, so it's a table constraint, not a database one). However, the constraint is quite complicated!—recall that it's supposed to mean "the average quantity of any given part, taken over all suppliers, can never decrease." No solution is provided here, because a proper formulation would require rather more apparatus than I've had room to describe in this short discussion; I'll have to ask you to take it on trust that the constraint can indeed be expressed in **Tutorial D,** as required. See reference [9] for further details.

# A Closer Look at Relational Databases

## 12

Now I've laid sufficient groundwork to begin homing in on one of the most fundamental questions of all—namely, what *is* a relational database, anyway? Lots of people think they know, but in fact not many do!

Well, of course, "everyone" does know that a relational database is a database that (so far as the user is concerned) contains *relations,* or more precisely *relvars*—and now I'll start using the more precise terminology of relations and relvars, rather than tables, for reasons that I hope will quickly become clear.

But what exactly is a relation?

Consider the figure overleaf, which shows a certain bill-of-materials relation that says, for example, that part P1 contains part P2 as a component, and it takes two P2's to make a P1. As the figure indicates, every relation has two parts or components, a *heading* and a *body*, where:

- The **heading** is a set of column-name:domain-name pairs, and

- The **body** is a set of rows that conform to that heading.

| MAJOR_P# : P# | MINOR_P# : P# | QTY : QTY |
|---|---|---|
| P1 | P2 | 2 |
| P1 | P3 | 4 |
| P2 | P3 | 1 |
| P2 | P4 | 3 |
| P3 | P5 | 9 |
| P4 | P5 | 8 |

heading—

A relation has a *heading* and a *body*

Also, of course, "everyone knows" that a relation can be pictured as a table, as in the figure. Note, however, that while it can indeed be *pictured* as a table, strictly speaking a relation is *not* a table. The term *relation* has a precise and somewhat abstract definition; the term *table,* by contrast, doesn't. (It could be given one, of course, but any such definition would always run the risk of being misunderstood, owing to the familiar but fuzzy meaning—or meanings, plural, rather—that the term already has.) Thus, a table in the relational world is best thought of as *a concrete picture of an abstract idea* (that abstract idea being a relation as such). And that picture, convenient though it is in informal contexts, does unfortunately suggest some things that aren't true. For example, it clearly suggests both (a) that the rows are in a certain top-to-bottom order and (b) that the columns are in a certain left-to-right order, neither of which is the case. (The rows and the columns of a relation both constitute mathematical *sets,* and sets in mathematics have no ordering to their elements.)

To repeat, the heading of a relation is a set of column-name:domain-name pairs. In the case of the bill-of-materials relation in the figure:

■ The column names are MAJOR_P# ("major part number"), MINOR_P# ("minor part number"), and QTY ("quantity").

■ The corresponding domain names are P# ("part number"), P# ("part number") again, and QTY ("quantity"), respectively.

- Each row includes a MAJOR_P# value (from the part number domain), a MINOR_P# value (also from the part number domain), and a QTY value (from the quantity domain).

Informally, of course, we often ignore the domain-name components of the heading, as in the next figure; thus, we often think of the heading, loosely, as just a set of column names.

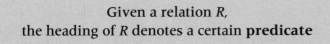

| MAJOR_P# | MINOR_P# | QTY |
|----------|----------|-----|
| P1 | P2 | 2 |
| P1 | P3 | 4 |
| P2 | P3 | 1 |
| P2 | P4 | 3 |
| P3 | P5 | 9 |
| P4 | P5 | 8 |

*note double-underline convention for primary key columns*

Just as an aside, note the convention for marking primary key columns—MAJOR_P# and MINOR_P#, in the example—with a double underline. (I used the same convention with the suppliers and parts database on Chapter 9, as you might have noticed.)

Now, there's a very important way of thinking about relations—it's not the way we usually do think about relations, but maybe it ought to be!—and that's as follows:

**Given a relation *R*,
the heading of *R* denotes a certain predicate**

A **predicate** is a *truth-valued function*. Like functions in general, a predicate takes a set of parameters; and when we substitute arguments for those parameters (in other words, when we invoke the function), we get a result, namely *true* or *false* (since the function is truth-valued). In the case of the bill-of-materials relation, for example, the predicate looks something like this:

The parameters are MAJOR_P#, QTY, and MINOR_P#, corresponding of course to the columns of the relation and standing for values from the relevant domains. And if we invoke this truth-valued function (if we "instantiate the predicate," as logicians say) and plug in argument values from the relevant domains for the parameters, then we get what logicians call a **proposition.** A proposition in logic is something that's either *true* or *false,* unequivocally. Thus, for example, if we plug in major part number P1, quantity 2, and minor part number P2, we get a proposition that's *true* (it's a "true fact" that part P1 contains 2 of part P2). By contrast, if we plug in, say, major part number P10, quantity 100, and minor part number P11, we get a proposition that's *false* (it's not the case—it's not a "true fact"—that part P10 contains 100 of part P11).

*And here comes the point:* The point is that—of course—the relation contains *all* and *only* the rows that correspond to *true* propositions. I'll say that again: The relation contains *exactly* "the true rows." Indeed, if a certain otherwise valid row does *not* appear, then we're entitled to assume that the corresponding proposition is *false.* In the example, the relation does not include the row (P10,P11,100); we're therefore entitled to assume that it is not the case that part P10 contains 100 of part P11. This state of affairs—the fact that the relation contains true rows, and we can assume that omitted ones are "false rows"—is known as *The Closed World Assumption,* or sometimes *The Closed World Interpretation.*

We can summarize all of this, somewhat loosely, as follows:

> **DOMAINS are sets of things we can talk about;**
>
> **RELATIONS are (true) statements about those things!**

To elaborate:

- *Domains* **comprise the things we can talk about.**

  In other words, domains give us our *vocabulary;* the things in domains are what we can make statements about. In the example, we have a domain of part numbers and a domain of quantities, so we can talk about part numbers, and we can talk about quantities, *and we can't talk about anything else.*

- *Relations* **comprise the truths we utter about those things.**

  Relations—or rows in relations, rather—are *what we say* about the things we can talk about; they're the true statements or assertions that we make about those things. In the example, we say it's a "true fact" that part P1 contains 2 of part P2, it's a "true fact" that part P2 contains 9 of part P5, and so on.

Given the foregoing, we can now note three very important corollaries:

1. Domains and relations are both necessary.

   This is the case because, without domains, we have nothing to talk about; without relations, we can't say anything. We *must* have both. (Of course, we all know that SQL products have historically been very weak in their support for domains. Nevertheless, we still need them, at least abstractly. When we're doing database design, we certainly have to think about domains, even if the target system doesn't give us very much direct support for them.)

2. Domains and relations aren't the same thing.

   There's a major difference between domains and relations, as in fact should be obvious. Beware anyone who tries to tell you otherwise! (Believe it or not, there are indeed some products on the market today that do try to pretend that domains and relations are the same kind of thing. This isn't the place to get into details, but I'm sure you can see that a product with such a massive confusion at its very heart is headed for deep trouble.)

**3.** Domains and relations are all we need.

Between them, domains and relations are sufficient, as well as necessary. *We can represent absolutely any information whatsoever exclusively in terms of domains and relations.* We don't need anything else. (Of course, I'm talking here about the *logical level.* We certainly need other constructs at the *physical* level, for performance reasons—but there's absolutely no good reason why those other constructs need be exposed to the user at the logical level.)

Let me editorialize here for a few moments. The fact is, a database, despite the name, isn't really just a collection of data. Rather, it's a collection of *propositions,* propositions that are understood by convention to be true. Thus, a database is really a formal logical system! It was Codd's very great insight, when he originally invented the relational model [4], to realize that databases could be perceived in such a way. (I don't think he ever stated the fact in so many words, but that's basically what he did.) As a consequence, the whole apparatus of formal logic becomes available for attacking "the database problem"—that is to say, for addressing questions such as the following:

- What should a query look like?
- What should the result of a query look like?
- How can we implement queries efficiently?
- How should we do logical database design?

And many others.

There's a very nice analogy (due to Hugh Darwen) that holds here and might help you appreciate and remember these important points:

> ***Domains are to relations as nouns are to sentences.***

After all, in natural language, nouns serve as our vocabulary—they denote the things we talk about. And sentences are what we say about the things we can talk about.

All right: So now you know (if perhaps you didn't before) what a relation really is and what relational databases really are. In the next chapter, we'll go on to consider the related question of what relations and relational databases really *mean*.

# What Relations Mean

# 13

❖ ❖ ❖

This chapter is *still* concerned with laying groundwork, but we're gradually getting closer to our real goal, which is, you will recall, to see how business rule technology is indeed in the spirit of the original relational wisdom. As I say, we're getting there, but I have one more groundwork topic to cover first: namely, the question of *meaning*. What do relations mean?

Well, first of all, it's surely obvious that every relation—be it a base relation, or a view, or a snapshot, or a final result, or an intermediate result, or any other kind of relation—certainly does have a meaning. And users need to know those meanings in order to use the database effectively, and efficiently. In the case of the suppliers relation from the suppliers and parts database, for example, the meaning is something like this:

*The supplier with the specified supplier number (that's the S# value) has the specified name (that's the SNAME value) and status (that's the STATUS value) and is located in the specified city (that's the CITY value). Moreover, the status value is in the range 0 to 100 inclusive, and must be 20 if the city is London. Also, no two suppliers have the same supplier number.*

*Informal meaning of the suppliers relation*

*Note:* This statement is neither precise nor complete, but it'll do for present purposes.

Observe now that the foregoing meaning can be regarded, once again, as a *predicate*. And, of course, at any given time, relation S—more precisely, *relvar* S—contains exactly the rows that make that predicate true (loosely speaking).

Before going any further, I should say that I've deliberately slurred over the difference between relation values and relation variables in the foregoing, somewhat. What's more, I'm going to continue doing the same thing over the next few pages. This isn't a very formal presentation! As Bertrand Russell once memorably remarked: "Writing can be either readable or precise, but not at the same time."

Anyway, the reason this question of meaning is so important is that, of course, the meaning of a given relation—that is, the predicate for that relation—is **the criterion for acceptability of updates** on that relation (or relvar, rather). Obviously, an update shouldn't be permitted if it violates the corresponding predicate.

In an ideal world, therefore, the DBMS would know the meaning of every relation, so that it could deal correctly with all possible updates. But, of course, that's impossible. There's no way it can know those meanings *exactly.* For example, there's no way the DBMS can know what it means for a certain supplier to be "in" a certain city or to "have" a certain status; these concepts are outside the system—they're understood by users, but not by the DBMS. More precisely, they're part of what logicians call the *interpretation* (of the relation in question).

What's more, suppose the user tries to insert a new supplier row, say the row (S6,Smith,50,Rome); in other words, the user is effectively asserting that it's a "true fact" that now there's a new supplier S6, with name Smith and status 50 and located in Rome. Then, again, there's no way the DBMS can possibly know whether that "true fact" is really true or not. All it can do is make sure the new row doesn't violate any of the known and applicable integrity constraints. If it doesn't, then the system will accept the new row and enter it into the database, *and will treat it as a "true fact" from that point forward.*

So the DBMS does not, and cannot, know the suppliers predicate 100 percent. But (as already indicated) it does know a good approximation!—it knows the *integrity constraints.* So we define the **formal** "meaning" of any given relation (sorry, relvar) to be the logical AND of all constraints that apply to the relation in question. (I'll come back and explain what I mean by that qualifier "formal" in just a moment.) For example, the formal meaning of the suppliers relation might look something like this:

*Formal meaning of the suppliers relation*

> **FORALL** *x#* **IN S#,** *xn* **IN NAME,** *xt* **IN INTEGER,** *xc* **IN CHAR,**
>          *y#* **IN S#,** *yn* **IN NAME,** *yt* **IN INTEGER,** *yc* **IN CHAR**
>   **( IF**
>         **{ S#** *x#,* **SNAME** *xn,* **STATUS** *xt,* **CITY** *xc* **} IN S AND**
>         **{ S#** *y#,* **SNAME** *yn,* **STATUS** *yt,* **CITY** *yc* **} IN S**
>   **THEN**
>         **(** $xt \geq 0$ **AND** $xt \leq 100$ **) AND**
>         **( IF** $xc =$ **'London' THEN** $xt = 20$ **) AND**
>         **( IF** $x\# = y\#$ **THEN** $xn = yn$ **AND** $xt = yt$ **AND** $xc = yc$ **) )**

This expression is the logical AND of the constraints we showed for suppliers in Chapter 12—the status is in the range 0 to 100 inclusive, supplier numbers are unique, and so on. (By the way, there's really no need for you to struggle through and try to understand this formal expression in every last detail.) And then we call this expression the **relation predicate** (or, more accurately, the *relvar* predicate) for suppliers.

In general, then, the relation predicate for a given relation represents the *formal, internal, system-understood* "meaning" of the relation in question—as opposed to the informal, external, *user*-understood meaning (what we called the "interpretation" above). The formal meaning can be thought of as an approximation to the informal meaning, but the whole point is that it *is* formal, and it's "understood" by the system. And, of course, it's that formal meaning that the system checks when updates are attempted. Indeed, as we already know, it's checked *immediately* when updates are attempted; to say it another way, relation predicates are satisfied *at statement boundaries*. This fact is so important that we call it *The Golden Rule:*

### The Golden Rule

*No update statement is ever allowed to leave any relation in a state that violates its own predicate.*

Now, I've been making a tacit assumption in the discussion so far that the relations we're talking about are all base relations specifically. But, of course, it isn't just base relations that are subject to update, as we know. In particular, views are updatable too, and so *The Golden Rule* applies to them as well. Thus, in order to decide whether an attempted update on a view is acceptable, the DBMS needs to know what the relation predicate is for that view. So what is the relation predicate for a view? Clearly, we need some *inference rules*—rules, that is, such that, if the system knows the predicates for the base relations, it can infer the predicates for the views.* *Note:* Of course, the system does know the predicates for the base relations— they're essentially the integrity constraints that were stated explicitly for those base relations when those base relations were defined.

---

*The inference rules we're talking about here are ones that are built into the relational model itself—they're not "business-specific" inference rules like the ones we discussed in Part I of this book.

It turns out that the required inference rules are very easy to state: They follow directly from the definitions of the applicable relational operators. For example:

- If view $C$ is defined as the union $A$ UNION $B$ of base relations $A$ and $B$, then the predicate $PC$ for $C$ is just $(PA)$ OR $(PB)$, where $PA$ and $PB$ are the predicates for $A$ and $B$, respectively. In other words, a row appears in $C$ if and only if it appears in $A$ or $B$ or both; so it must satisfy $PA$ or $PB$ or both. The implications for updates on $C$ are obvious.

- Likewise, the predicate for the intersection $A$ INTERSECT $B$ is $(PA)$ AND $(PB)$; the predicate for the difference $A$ MINUS $B$ is $(PA)$ AND NOT $(PB)$; and so on.

Incidentally, I'd like to point out as an aside that it's this business of predicates that's the key to the whole question of view updating. I mentioned in Chapter 10 that views are always updatable (barring integrity constraint violations); well, it was the business of predicates that I had in mind when I said that, as I hope you can now see.

As another aside, I think it's also worth pointing out that the overall database has a predicate too, and hence a formal meaning too. As we know, a database is a named container for relations; and those relations have formal meanings, as we've seen. So the **database predicate** is the logical AND of all applicable constraints—which is to say, the logical AND of all relation predicates and all database constraints that apply to that database, loosely speaking. And the database predicate too is satisfied at statement boundaries (that is, *The Golden Rule* applies to the overall database as well as to the individual relations in that database).

One last point: Of course, the term "database" as I'm using it here denotes a purely *logical* concept; it's the database as perceived by the user. I'm certainly not talking about any kind of *physical* construct at the physical storage level. In the extreme, one "database," in my sense of the term, might map to any number of physically stored databases, managed by any number of different DBMSs, running on any number of different machines, supported by any number of different operating systems, and connected together by any number of different communication networks.

# Business Rules and the Relational Model

# 14

Now at last I can get to the real point of this part of the book and consider what relationship might exist between business rules and all of these relational ideas we've been discussing in the last few chapters.

The net of what I've been saying in those last few chapters is basically that the DBMS needs to know certain integrity constraints—which is to say, certain business rules—in order for it to be able to "do updating right" (and this remark is equally as true of views as it is of base relations). And that's why those business rules really ought to be part of the data model!—in order to make them known to the DBMS. ("Data model" here is to be understood in its second sense, of course.)

In my opinion, this is a place where the SQL vendors *really* let us down. (I've mentioned several ways now in which the SQL vendors let us down, but this one is perhaps the biggest; indeed, it underlies many of the others.) And it's precisely because of this failure on the part of the SQL vendors—the failure for so long to provide anything even close to satisfactory support for integrity constraints—that separate rule engines are important in practice, of course. (Though, to be fair, as I pointed out in Chapter 7, there are also some positive advantages to be gained from supporting the rules in a separate software component: DBMS independence, the possibility of spanning DBMSs, possibly other advantages as well. So am I arguing out of both sides of my mouth here? No, not really, as I hope to show in a few moments.)

I think it's interesting to take a moment and speculate about just why the SQL vendors did let us down in this regard. Here's one possible reason. In an interview he did for *Data Base Newsletter* in May/June 1997 [20], Gary Morgenthaler, previously CEO of Ingres Corp. and later of Illustra Information Technologies, Inc., said the following (the italics are mine):

> **[At] Ingres, and more recently at Illustra . . . , we pursued developments in the direction of . . . a more declarative rule structure. The problem, as always, was in being pulled in many different directions at the same time.** *Issues such as declarative rule support end up taking a back seat to other, more pressing database market concerns.*
>
> **—Gary Morgenthaler**

It seems to me that the "database market," if that term is meant to include customers as well as vendors, doesn't always act in its own best interests! Certainly it's hard to imagine what "database market concerns" could or should be more "pressing" than making sure that databases and applications are correct.

Anyway, let's get back to business rules and integrity constraints. The big point I want to make is this. As far as I'm concerned, the process of doing logical database design and constructing the data model is *precisely* a matter of pinning down the applicable business rules (or *constraints,* or *predicates,* or whatever you prefer to call them). Thus, what I do when I do database design is as follows:

- First of all, I try to decide what the relevant *vocabulary* is. What are the things we need to talk about? They might be supplier numbers, part numbers, weights, quantities, cities (and so on and so forth). In other words, I try to pin down the *domains,* including the applicable *domain constraints* (which are, of course, basically just the domain *definitions,* or specifications of the legal values for the domain in question).

■ Next, I write down what might be called the *base predicates* or *base constraints*—for example, "supplier S# is located in city CITY," "status values are in the range 0 to 100 inclusive," "supplier numbers are unique" (and so on and so forth). Those base predicates map to *base relations* and associated formal *constraints* (relvar constraints, to be exact).

■ Then I write down the *database constraints*—those constraints that span base relations (especially foreign key constraints, a pragmatically important special case).

■ Then I specify certain *views* (possibly other derived relations—for example, snapshots—as well). I'll come back and say a little more about views later in this chapter.

■ Then I iterate . . . The entire process is highly iterative, of course, as everybody is well aware.

What I don't do is draw "E/R diagrams"!* ("E/R" is short for *entity/relationship,* as I'm sure you know, and the process of drawing E/R diagrams is sometimes referred to as *E/R modeling.*) Although E/R diagrams can be useful for explicating the structure of the database at a high intuitive level— and of course you're free to make use of them for that purpose if you want—the trouble is that they're virtually incapable of representing integrity constraints (except for a few special cases, including foreign key constraints in particular, that are admittedly important in practice). And as far as I'm concerned, by contrast, database design is really all about specifying integrity constraints! Database design **is** constraint definition.

---

*At least, I don't do this exclusively, or even primarily.

I'll have a little more to say about E/R modeling in a few moments. First, however, I'd like to revisit one of the constraints from the credit limit example that we looked at in Part I of this book: "A customer's total owed can't be greater than that customer's credit limit." You might recall that we needed several business rules to express this constraint when we considered it in Chapter 2. Well, you probably won't be surprised by now to learn that it can be expressed *as a single statement* in a language like **Tutorial D**—see Chapter 11—that's true to the relational model. It might go like this:

```
WITH QTY_ORD * ORD_PRICE AS LINE_ITEM_AMOUNT ,
     Sum ( LINE_ITEM_AMOUNT ) AS ORDER_TOTAL ,
     Sum ( ORDER_TOTAL where not PAID ) AS TOTAL_OWED
     TOTAL_OWED ≤ CREDIT_LIMIT ;
```

The syntax here is somewhat simplified, of course, but so it was in the "business rules" version in Chapter 2 as well. Note the use of a "WITH clause" to introduce names for expressions. Overall, the structure of the statement is basically as follows:

```
[ WITH <expression> AS <name>
   [, <expression> AS <name> ... ] : ]
  <conditional expression> ;
```

The optional WITH clause introduces shorthand names for the specified expressions, and the conditional expression then defines the constraint *per se* in terms of those introduced names. In the example, therefore, the first line defines LINE_ITEM_AMOUNT to be the product of the quantity ordered and the order price; the second line defines ORDER_TOTAL to be the sum of such line item amounts; the third line defines TOTAL_OWED as the sum of unpaid order totals; finally, the fourth line specifies the actual constraint (the total owed must not exceed the credit limit).

*Note:* The fact that the entire rule can be expressed as a single statement doesn't mean it has to be, of course; it can just as well be expressed in the form of several smaller statements, as it was in Chapter 2.

By way of another example, here in outline is the reorder example from Chapter 2 (which, if you remember, was a "stimulus/response" rule—it took the form of a "triggering action" plus a "triggered event"). For simplicity, I've omitted the details of the WITH clause this time.

```
WITH ... :
    IF QTY_ON_HAND — QTY_ORD < REORDER_LEVEL
    THEN CALL REORDER ( ... ) ;
```

("If the remaining quantity on hand is less than the reorder level, then invoke a procedure to carry out the necessary reordering.")

As these examples should make clear, business rules really are very much in keeping with *The Original Relational Vision.* Codd's very first paper on the relational model [4]— it was an IBM Research Report, with a publication date of August 19th, 1969 (over 30 years ago!)—was entitled "Derivability, Redundancy, and Consistency of Relations Stored in Large Data Banks." Observe, therefore, that Codd was talking about—indeed, emphasizing—consistency, or in other words integrity constraints, right at the very outset of "the relational era," over 30 years ago. (He was also emphasizing derivability and redundancy, both of which are also highly pertinent to business rules.)

In like manner, the very first edition of my book *An Introduction to Database Systems* [7], which was written in 1972, included the following sentence: "Each relation [has] a set of integrity constraints." Those constraints constitute what we now know as the relation predicate, of course.

To say it one more time, then: In an ideal world, business rules such as the ones just shown would indeed be part of the data model—there wouldn't be any artificial dividing line between the two—and they would be supported directly by the DBMS.

What's more, *view definitions* are inference rules! For example, recall the following inference rule from Chapter 4:

```
IF TOTAL_PAID(c) > 100K THEN GOOD_CUSTOMER(c)
```

("if customer *c* has paid more than $100,000 in total, then customer *c* is a good customer"). As pointed out in Chapter 4, this rule is effectively the definition of what constitutes a "good customer." And here's a relational equivalent of that definition (expressed in SQL this time, not **Tutorial D,** for reasons of familiarity):

```
CREATE VIEW GOOD_CUSTOMER AS
       SELECT *
       FROM   CUSTOMER
       WHERE  TOTAL_PAID > 100K ;
```

This view definition is precisely a definition of "good customers"; the system will automatically treat a given customer as "good" if and only if that customer has paid more than $100,000 in total. To say it again, therefore, view definitions are basically inference rules, and it follows that the data model (which I certainly take to include view definitions) can handle inference rules too: trivially so, in fact.

Now, I promised a little while back that I'd come back and say a little more about "E/R modeling." I claimed earlier that E/R modeling is incapable of dealing with integrity constraints, except for a few special cases. In particular, as John Sowa has observed [27], it can't handle the *quantifiers* (and almost all integrity constraints—arguably *all* integrity constraints—involve quantifiers). Since the quantifiers were invented (by Frege) in 1879, this failure makes E/R modeling, as Sowa puts it, "a pre-1879 kind of logic" (!).

Further support for the position that drawing pictures isn't necessarily the best way to do database design is provided by Terry Moriarty in reference [22], where she says:

> Declarative rules are too complex to be captured as part of the business model and must be defined separately.

(From the context, it's clear that by "the business model" here Moriarty means *pictures,* and by "defining declarative rules" she means *specifying constraints.* And I say again that, as far as I'm concerned, database design is *precisely* a process of "specifying constraints.")

More evidence: In reference [13], Terry Halpin describes a query language called ConQuer that "enables users to pose queries in a readily understandable way"—in effect, by drawing pictures. He claims, probably with justification, that ConQuer is much more user-friendly than SQL. However, he also says the following:

> Although [ConQuer's] graphical notation can capture more business rules than [E/R diagrams], it still needs to be supplemented by a textual language [for expressing certain constraints].

And in a more recent article [14], Halpin also comments on the shortcomings of UML (UML = Unified Modeling Language) in the same connection:

> UML does not require conceptual identification schemes for its classes . . . and does not even include a standard notation for saying that attribute values must be unique for their class. [*Two very important kinds of constraints here!*] However, UML does allow user-defined constraints to be added in braces or notes *in whatever language users wish* [*my italics*].

He goes on to demonstrate that UML diagrams are unsatisfactory as a representation of both external and internal relation predicates. One further quote:

> UML's weakness with regard to [representing external predicates] carries over into its [support for] constraints and derivation rules. [In fact, it suggests] that OCL (Object Constraint Language) be used for formal expression of such rules [*in other words, the diagrams need to be supplemented with rules expressed in the form of text*].

All of the foregoing might go some way toward explaining the sorry *status quo*, perhaps. To be more precise, the fact that SQL products have been so bad for so long at supporting constraints might be because database designers typically *don't* regard constraints as the foundation of the data model, treating them instead as subsequent add-ons, and so haven't exerted the necessary pressure on the vendors. If these speculations are close to the mark, then it seems to me that E/R modeling and similar diagramming techniques have a lot to answer for! See reference [23] for further discussion of this point and many related ones.

I'd like to close this chapter with a couple of final points. The first is a quote to buttress my claim that business rules are in keeping with the spirit of the relational model. It's from Gary Morgenthaler again, from the same interview as before [20]:

> **As an enabler of consistent, sharable implementation of business logic, rules portend a second major revolution in the integration of systems—the first being the introduction of relational DBMS products. Rules also might be seen as finally delivering on a long-unfulfilled promise of the first revolution—the ability to move data integrity enforcement out of application programs and into a location from which it can be [applied] across all applications consistently.**
>
> **—Gary Morgenthaler**

I don't think I need add anything to these remarks.

My second point is this. Recall the following figure from Chapter 5:

*Rule engine vs. DBMS*

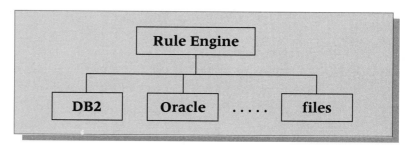

As the figure indicates, in today's business rule systems, the rule engine is a separate software component, independent of the DBMS and running on top of the DBMS, instead of being integrated with the DBMS as I've been arguing it really ought to be. However, I did also point out, both in Chapter 5 and in Chapter 7, that such independence could actually be an advantage. So—as I put it a few pages back—was I arguing out of both sides of my mouth?

Well, of course I don't think I was. You see, there's another way to look at the arrangement in the figure. To be specific, we can think of the rule engine **as** a DBMS, one that exists at a higher level and simply happens to store its data behind the scenes using DB2, Oracle, and the rest! Note in particular that, under this interpretation, the problem with *loss of independence* goes away. That is, the fact that the business rules are "handled by the DBMS" doesn't mean we're dependent on DB2 or Oracle or whatever—rather, we're dependent on that "higher-level DBMS" (to wit, the rule engine) only, and *that* DBMS is independent of all the rest.

One final point to close the chapter (a small one, but it might help you understand the shift in perspective that I've just proposed): The fact is, there's a clear parallel between the rule engine and existing "data access middleware" such as IBM's DataJoiner product [1]. Like the rule engine, DataJoiner is really a higher-level DBMS (as a matter of fact, it actually contains a copy of IBM's DB2 product); and like the rule engine, DataJoiner just happens to store its data under the covers using other DBMSs (and/or "legacy" file systems, of course, a possibility also mentioned in Chapter 5 and illustrated in the figure).

# Summary of Part II

# 15

By way of conclusion, let me summarize the argument I've
been trying to make in this second part of the book. Basically,
I've tried to convince you that business rules are truly in
keeping with the spirit of the original relational wisdom; in
effect, I wanted to try and persuade you that they're "intellec-
tually respectable" and do rely on a good solid body of theory.
In order to do that, I spent most of the time explaining certain
aspects of the relational model that—I'm sorry to say—aren't
as widely understood or appreciated as they ought to be. And,
of course, it's precisely those aspects of the relational model
that constitute that "good solid body of theory."

First of all, in Chapter 9, I talked about values and
variables in general, and relation values and variables (relvars)
in particular. These concepts are certainly logically distinct
and—in precise discussions, at least—it's a good idea to keep
them rigidly apart, though I deliberately didn't try to be so
precise myself in all of my own discussions.

Then, in Chapter 10, I took a look at views, base tables,
and stored tables, and I explained that base tables as well as
views are a logical concept, not a physical one. Base tables
should NOT map one-to-one to stored tables!—there should
be at least as much variability possible between base and
stored tables as there can between views and base tables.
Also, views are logically updatable, like base tables; indeed,
if base tables can map to stored tables in arbitrary ways but

are updatable, then it follows that views, which map to base tables in arbitrary ways, must be logically updatable too (the two problems are logically one and the same, but manifested at two distinct points in the overall architecture of the system).

Next, in Chapter 11, I introduced a taxonomy for integrity constraints, dividing them into domain (or type) constraints, column (or attribute) constraints, table (or relvar) constraints, and database constraints. They're all important, but relation constraints are perhaps the most important for our purposes. Well, and database constraints, of course. Oh, and type constraints too . . . In fact, of course, they're all important, each in their own way.

That discussion of integrity constraints then allowed me to get into the question of what a database truly is. It's not just a repository for data; rather, it's really a collection of *true propositions.* And those propositions are true instantiations of the *predicates* that correspond to the relations. And I showed how domains and relations were both *necessary* and *sufficient* to represent absolutely anything we want to represent, at least at the logical level.

And that discussion in turn led me into the question of what relations mean. Every relation has a *relation predicate,* representing the formal meaning of the relation in question; and that formal relation predicate, which is the logical AND of the constraints that apply to the relation in question, is *the criterion for acceptability of updates* on that relation. Remember *The Golden Rule*—no update statement is ever allowed to leave any relation (or relvar, rather) in a state that violates its own predicate.

Finally, in Chapter 14, I claimed that the whole subject of integrity constraints and predicates was really business rules by another name! In other words, business rules really do fit very well as an integral part of the relational model. The trouble is, they're exactly the part of the relational model that the "relational" vendors—or the SQL vendors, rather—really haven't done a very good of supporting in the past. How agreeable, then, to be able to report that the industry is finally doing something to repair that major historical omission.

# References and
# Bibliography

❖  ❖  ❖

1. Charles J. Bontempo and C. M. Saracco: "Data Access Middleware: Seeking out the Middle Ground," *InfoDB 9*, No. 4 (August 1995).

2. Stefano Ceri and Jennifer Widom: "Deriving Production Rules for Constraint Maintenance," Proc. 16th Int. Conf. on Very Large Data Bases, Brisbane, Australia (August 1990).

3. J. Craig Cleaveland: *An Introduction to Data Types.* Reading, Mass.: Addison-Wesley (1986).

4. E. F. Codd: "Derivability, Redundancy, and Consistency of Relations Stored in Large Data Banks," IBM Research Report RJ599 (August 19th, 1969). *Note:* See also (a) the revised (and more widely distributed) version of this paper, entitled "A Relational Model of Data for Large Shared Data Banks," *CACM 13,* No. 6 (June 1970), republished in "Milestones of Research," *CACM 26,* No. 1 (January 1982); (b) references [7], [8], and [9].

5. E. F. Codd: "Extending the Database Relational Model to Capture More Meaning," *ACM Transactions on Database Systems 4,* No. 4 (December 1979).

6. C. J. Date: "The Extended Relational Model RM/T," in C. J. Date, *Relational Database Writings 1991–1994.* Reading, Mass.: Addison-Wesley (1995).

7. C. J. Date: *An Introduction to Database Systems* (7th edition). Reading, Mass.: Addison-Wesley (2000). *Note:* The first edition of this book, referenced in Chapter 14 of the present book, had a copyright date of 1975 but was written in 1972.

8. C. J. Date: *The Database Relational Model: A Retrospective Review and Analysis.* Reading, Mass.: Addison-Wesley (2000, to appear).

9. C. J. Date and Hugh Darwen: *Foundation for Future Database Systems: The Third Manifesto* (2nd edition). Reading, Mass.: Addison-Wesley (2000, to appear).

10. C. J. Date and David McGoveran, "Updating Union, Intersection, and Difference Views" and "Updating Joins and Other Views," both in C. J. Date: *Relational Database Writings 1991–1994.* Reading, Mass.: Addison-Wesley (1995). *Note:* These two papers provide an informal sketch of the theory of view updating. Sadly, they're both a little out of date by now and in need of some revision, while the *formal* description is still in preparation.

11. C. J. Date (with Colin J. White): *A Guide to DB2* (4th edition). Reading, Mass.: Addison-Wesley (1992).

12. GUIDE Business Rules Project: *Final Report,* revision 1.2 (October 1997).

13. Terry Halpin: "Conceptual Queries," *Data Base Newsletter 26,* No. 2 (March/April 1998).

14. Terry Halpin: "The Case for Data Use Cases," *Data To Knowledge Newsletter 27,* No. 6 (November/December 1999).

15. Val Huber: "Automating Business Rules" (interview), *Data Base Newsletter 25,* No. 2 (March/April 1997).

16. International Organization for Standardization (ISO): *Database Language SQL,* Document ISO/IEC 9075:1999. Also available as American National Standards Institute (ANSI) Document ANSI NCITS.135-1999. *Note:* The original monolithic document is in the process of being replaced by an open-ended series of separate "Parts" (ISO 9075-1, -2, etc.), under the general title *Information Technology—Database Languages—SQL.* So far the following Parts have been defined:

    Part 1: Framework (SQL/Framework)
    Part 2: Foundation (SQL/Foundation)
    Part 3: Call-Level Interface (SQL/CLI)
    Part 4: Persistent Stored Modules (SQL/PSM)
    Part 5: Host Language Bindings (SQL/Bindings)
    Part 6: XA Specialization (SQL/Transaction)
    Part 7: Temporal (SQL/Temporal)
    Part 8: *There is no Part 8*
    Part 9: Management of External Data (SQL/MED)
    Part 10: Object Language Bindings (SQL/OLB)

17. Jonathan J. King: "QUIST: A System for Semantic Query Optimization in Relational Databases," Proc. 7th Int. Conf. on Very Large Data Bases, Cannes, France (September 1981).

18. Raymond A. Lorie and Bradford W. Wade: "The Compilation of a High-Level Data Language," IBM Research Report RJ2598 (August 1979).

19. James Martin and James J. Odell: *Object-Oriented Methods: A Foundation* (2nd edition). Englewood Cliffs, N.J.: Prentice-Hall (1997).

20. Gary Morgenthaler: "Business Rule Automation" (interview), *Data Base Newsletter 25,* No. 3 (May/June 1997).

21. Gary Morgenthaler: Private communication (July 9th, 1999).

22. Terry Moriarty: *Enterprise View* (regular column), *DBP&D 10,* No. 8 (August 1997).

23. G. M. Nijssen, D. J. Duke, and S. M. Twine: "The Entity-Relationship Data Model Considered Harmful," Proc. 6th Symposium on Empirical Foundations of Information and Software Sciences, Atlanta, Ga. (October 1988). *Note:* A *précis* of this paper can be found in reference [7].

24. Ronald G. Ross: *Business Rule Concepts.* Business Rule Solutions LLC, 2476 Bolsover St. #488, Houston, TX 77005 (1998).

25. Ronald G. Ross: *The Business Rule Book: Classifying, Defining, and Modeling Rules* (2nd edition). Business Rule Solutions LLC, 2476 Bolsover St. #488, Houston, TX 77005 (1997).

26. L. A. Rowe and K. Shoens: "A Forms Application Development System," Proc. 1982 ACM SIGMOD International Conference on Management of Data, Orlando, Fla. (June 1982).

27. J. F. Sowa: *Conceptual Structures: Information Processing in Mind and Machine.* Reading, Mass.: Addison-Wesley (1984). *Note:* The remarks attributed to Sowa in Chapter 14 are not taken directly from this book; rather, they're taken from a live presentation by Sowa in or around 1990 on the application of the "conceptual structures" described in this book to data modeling specifically.

28. D. Teichroew: "Automation of System Building," *Datamation 17,* No. 16 (August 15th, 1971).

29. Stanley B. Zdonik and David Maier: "Fundamentals of Object-Oriented Databases," in Stanley B. Zdonik and David Maier (eds.): *Readings in Object-Oriented Database Systems.* San Francisco, Calif.: Morgan Kaufmann (1990).

# Index

entity, 10, 36
entity/relationship, *see* E/R
executable specifications, 5
existence dependency, 10
existential quantifier, *see*
    EXISTS
EXISTS, 32
extensibility, 42

firing (rules), 15
FORALL, 32
foreign key, 10, 18, 23
form, 4
form transition, 22
Frege, Gottlob, 118

*Golden Rule,* 110

Halpin, Terry, 119
HAS A constraint, 95, 96
heading, 99
Huber, Val, 8, 65

immediate checking, 90, 92,
    94
implementation, 34
inference rule, 29
    relational model, 110–111
    same as view definition,
      117–118
inheritance, 89, 90
integrity constraint, 26ff
interpretation (relation), 108
Irvine, Paul, 19, 48
IS A constraint, 89, 96

Java, 9, 57

kernel entity, 95

levels of abstraction, *see*
    abstraction
Lorie, Raymond, 55–56

"materialized view," 82–83
middleware, 38, 70, 120–121
Morgenthaler, Gary, 17, 53–54,
    114, 120
Moriarty, Terry, 118
multi-row constraint, 31, 93
multi-table constraint, 32, 93

Odell, James, 25
optimization, 15, 39, 56
    semantic, 48–50
ordering independence, 17

partitioning code, 39
performance, 55–56, 85–86
    *vs.* integrity, 85
possible representation, *see*
    POSSREP
POSSREP, 88
predicate, 101, 108
predicate logic, 56
presentation, 6
    services, 7
primary key, 92
procedural, 5
productivity, 50–51
proposition, 102

QBF, 4
quantifier, *see* EXISTS; FORALL
Query By Forms, *see* QBF

relation assignment, 77
relation predicate, 109
relation value, 75ff
relation variable, 75ff
relation *vs.* domain, *see* domain
    *vs.* relation
relation *vs.* table, *see* table *vs.*
    relation
relationship, 95
relvar, 78
relvar predicate, *see* relation
    predicate

# Addison-Wesley Professional

## How to Register Your Book

### Register this Book

Visit: **http://www.aw.com/cseng/register**

Enter the ISBN*

Then you will receive:

- Notices and reminders about upcoming author appearances, tradeshows, and onlin[e] chats with special guests
- Advanced notice of forthcoming editions of your book
- Book recommendations
- Notification about special contests and promotions throughout the year

*The ISBN can be found on the copyright page of the book

### Visit our Web site

http://www.aw.com/cseng

When you think you've read enough, there's always more content for you at Addison-Wesley's web site. Our web site contains a directory of complete product information including:

- Chapters
- Exclusive author interviews
- Links to authors' pages
- Tables of contents
- Source code

You can also discover what tradeshows and conferences Addison-Wesley will be attending, read what others are saying about our titles, and find out where and when you can meet our authors and have them sign your book.

We encourage you to patronize the many fine retailers who stock Addison-Wesley titles. Visit our online directory to find stores near you.

### Contact Us via Ema[il]

**cepubprof@awl.co[m]**
Ask general questions about our boo[ks]
Sign up for our electronic mailing lis[t]
Submit corrections for our web si[te]

**mikeh@awl.co[m]**
Submit a book propos[al]
Send errata for a bo[ok]

**cepubpublicity@awl.co[m]**
Request a review copy for a member of the me[dia]
interested in reviewing new tit[les]

**registration@awl.co[m]**
Request information about book registrati[on]

## Addison-Wesley Professional

**One Jacob Way, Reading, Massachusetts 01867 USA**

TEL 781-944-3700 • FAX 781-942-3076